The Experience of God

THE EXPERIENCE OF GOD

Outlines for a Contemporary Spirituality

CHARLES M. MAGSAM, M.M.

ORBIS BOOKS • MARYKNOLL, NEW YORK

Contents

Introduction   3

I: COMMUNITARIAN

1. Common Service to God and Man   9
2. Social Factors Which Influence
     the Experience of God in Community   20
3. The Value of the Human Person   31
4. Our First Vocation Is to Be Our Distinctive Selves   38
5. Freedom and Responsibility in Community   44
6. Initiative and Collegiality   52

II: BIBLICAL

7. Jesus Is Lord   69
8. Jesus Is Our Covenant   78
9. The Blood of the Covenant   87
10. The Holy Spirit Empowers Us to Live the Covenant   98

III: PRAYERFUL

11. Our Natural Need to Pray   109
12. Covenant Prayer Is Prophetic Prayer   119
13. Fellowship and Joy in Prayer   128
14. Towards Contemplative Prayer   143

IV: SERVICE-ORIENTATED

15. Mutual Tolerance   157
16. Active Listening in Human Encounter   166
17. Service through Supportive Teamwork   175
18. Serving Christ and Our Brothers and Sisters   183

V: AFFECTIVE

19. The Total Person Involved in the Experience of God   195
20. Personality Balance and Self-Realization   202
21. Friendship and Community   212
22. Committed Celibacy in Spiritual Leaders   222

VI: CONCLUSION

23. The Prophetic Role of the
     Redeemed Christian in a Secular World   233

The Experience of God

Introduction

History indicates clearly that wherever the religious system of a culture has disintegrated, the consequences to the life of the people have been disastrous. So intimate is the connection of religious belief and practice with the environment that the decline of the former lays waste to the latter. Moreover, it is impossible to supplant one religion by another unless the environment itself changes basically.

In our time social changes are very rapid, and they are proceeding largely without religious influence. The worst of it is that these changes are destroying the religious values of the past without replacing them with new beliefs, so that those writers are being very precise who describe our society as post-Christian. Nevertheless the religious structures which entered into the formation of our culture remain, and also, working as a leaven, the Christian community which Christ promised to be with until the end of time. Moreover, outside the boundaries of the Christian community, insofar as we can define them in this life, are the men who in every age, whether consciously or unconsciously, are in search of that ultimate mystery, transcending time and change, which we call God.

To speak of the experience of God is to enter upon a subject which is of its nature open-ended, for the aspect of divinity which is experienced depends variously upon temperament, personality, circumstances, cultural formation. Among the Hindus of the Far East, for example, the master gives each young man a personal name for God, e.g., Beloved, Creator, Unity, Protector, which becomes his pathway to prayer and encounter with God. The temperament, needs, and capabilities of the individual decide the name of God which is given to each one. He is strictly advised to keep this name as a personal secret, not sharing it even with his wife or with friends.

The experience of God may be described as a mental and affective awareness of a supreme personal being who is Creator and Center of all that is. But no sooner do we attempt even a descriptive definition than we must add that the experience of God defies definition because it is as distinctive in each person as each is distinctive from every other. Each man's experience of God is intensely personal and unique in its intuition and resonance, even though it is also social in each man's dependence for formation upon his fellow men and in its flowing out to them in attention, affection, and service. The experience may be as simple and mysterious as love or as bizarre as that of Wilkerson's harmonica player who said that God is "purple, violet squish." In any case, the distinctively personal could never be merely intellectual; it necessarily includes the entire personality, i.e., the physical, emotional, rational, the mystical and ecstatic. It is the whole person relating to total divinity.

Our concern in this book with the experience of God is both personal and social, but always practical, not speculative. Everyone has to be concerned about the social aspect of life, about his environment, because he is molded by it, and especially by his attitude towards it. "Unless man continually tries to shape and reshape his world, his relationships and the structures which condition or change them, he will never attain the full dimension of freedom."[1] But at the same time, changes of methods and structures are only patchwork and will accomplish little or nothing without a basic change in man's relationship with God. Only through a vital encounter with God will man find the right direction and the constant replenishment of his energies that is needed for the gradual transformation of what so deeply affects him. So our reflections on the experience of God will have the object of making possible that organic change of society which comes from within.

Although we shall draw freely on the spiritual literature of the world, we shall have particular reference to the sources from which the Christian community draws its sustenance: Scripture, the writing of the saints, the voice of tradition, as it is heard in the papal Encyclicals and the Councils. With regard to the dignity of the moral conscience, the Second Vatican Council writes:

> In the depths of his conscience, man detects a law which he does not impose upon himself, but which holds him to obedience. Always summoning him to love good and avoid evil, the voice of conscience can when necessary speak to his heart more specifically: do this, shun that. For man has in his heart a law written by God. To obey it is the very dignity of man; according to it he will be judged (cf. Rom 2:15-16). Conscience is the most secret core and sanctuary of a man. There he is alone with God, whose voice echoes in his depths. In a wonderful manner conscience reveals that law which is fulfilled by love of God and neighbor (cf. Mt 22:37-40; Gal 5:14). In fidelity to conscience Christians are joined with the rest of men in the search for truth, and for the genuine solution to the numerous problems which arise in the life of individuals and from social relationships.[2]

It is notable that in our day many people have abandoned the religious faith and practice of their parents. With respect to our youth, to a great extent, this relates to an unstable period of growth. Organized religion and God himself are representative of the authority against which the young are rebelling. As Father Andrew Greeley puts it: "The majority of the so-called religious crises of young adulthood have little to do with matters of doctrine and a lot to do with the transference of resentments against parents to God and the Church."[3] But the fact remains that in the parents themselves, even those who continue the practice of religion to some extent, there is an unease not known by earlier generations. This is inevitable in view of the intimate relation between religion and the environment. For as the environment undergoes radical change, the believer feels old certainties fading away. The Christian knows in his heart that the eternal truths are changeless; but as practices which were part of the past are stripped away to adapt the faith to a new age, he is conscious above all of a psychological void.

Therefore it is most encouraging that at the present time many people of all ages, but especially the young, are filling the religious vacuum in their lives by a rediscovery of Jesus as Savior and by a renewed interest in God's word in Scripture. They are experiencing God anew and at a very deep level, as they read the Bible and pray together in groups, large or small, and engage in private Scripture reading and prayer. There seems to be an increasing preference for the communal religious experience, and several chapters of this book are concerned with the way this can be implemented. The Biblical section explores in brief summary the scriptural sources of covenant prayer.

The Christian lives by faith and not by sight. Above all, this book is an attempt to outline those elements which go into the making of a mature Christian conscience. For just as, on the natural level, all human achievements rest on a capacity for taking risks, so with the life of faith. In this earthly life our beliefs, on the natural level, are a matter of the convergence of a great variety of probabilities. Faith is a risk, but everyone has to accept it. It is not necessary to know how probable a probability is before acting on it: that is the act of faith. As Newman says in his *Apologia pro Vita Sua*, "It is faith and love that give probability a force that it does not have of itself."

Let us go forth in faith, then, to the greatest adventure of which the human person is capable: the search for the experience of God.

[1] Bernard Haring, *Theology of Protest* (New York: Farrar, Straus and Giroux, 1970), p. 52.

[2] Pastoral Constitution on the Church in the Modern World, no. 16. *The Documents of Vatican II*, ed. Walter M. Abbott, S.J. (New York: America Press, 1966). Excerpts from the Constitutions and Decrees of the Ecumenical Council are taken from *The Documents of Vatican II*, published by the Guild Press, America Press, Association Press, and Herder and Herder, and copyrighted 1966 by the America Press. Used by permission.

[3] *The Crucible of Change* (New York: Sheed and Ward, 1968), p. 13.

I

Communitarian

CHAPTER 1

Common Service to God and Man

No man can live a truly human life in isolation, standing immobile and indifferent to the ebb and flow of life around him, for the need of society belongs to the essence of our human nature. Happily there is in our time a realistic moving away from the withdrawal, the defensive isolationism, the lonely heroism so frequent in the past, towards cooperation and mutual affective support in some kind of community.

We are made to grow and develop by a twofold process of expansion and assimilation. We need to go out of ourselves to be vitally in touch with the whole of reality, sensitively responsive to all the richness of being in persons and things. This means persons and things as they actually are, in their relation to God, to one another, and to the environment. From them, even while we are still giving of ourselves, we assimilate what we need for our personal development, growth, and fulfillment.

Intellectually we need community because, whereas we are in touch with the whole world through our mass communications, we cannot live the life of our intellect wholly in terms of continents and world movements. Owing to the inherent limitations of our nature, we need to reduce things to the concrete, the manageable, the bite-size—and therefore also to a community of human persons which we can experience. On the purely intellectual level, what we can know of God is really very little—and hence, in his wisdom, he revealed himself in concrete terms related to the community and the family: father, mother, sister, brother, friend.

Our need for community is an affective need as well; for we cannot live with mere abstractions—persons seen on a screen, encountered in a book, conceived in social theories, or experienced as moving objects in the neighborhood or even within the same four walls. We need a heart-to-heart relation with other people on a deep level of friendliness renewed by frequent contacts—with co-workers and neighbors as well as family and friends. We need this partly to remove a sense of threat which would be there if we had constantly to deal with the reactions of others as unknown factors; but we need it even more for the perfectly natural and good satisfaction of normal relationships with other people who equally have affective needs.

In other words, the sense of belonging to a group with whom we have mental and affective bonds, a group in which we feel accepted, is essential to us. We need to be able to depend on the group for support and know that we can count on its members for understanding and compassion in our sorrows and defeats; we need to be able to share with the group our successes and joys. And finally we need a significant role to play in the group, meaningful work to do. In the community my work becomes not my work but the work of the community, work for which I am responsible and want to be responsible as my expression of the love we have for one another.

From this it follows that any responsible human person wants to give to the group his free, intelligent, active cooperation in everything that touches the group. Living things which feed upon other living things are called parasites. It is a matter of experience that human parasites are led into frustration, unhappiness, alienation from self and very soon from the group. The fact is that the health of the community depends on love. Unless God is at the center of community, constantly replenishing the energies and renewing the meaning of love, mere human efforts easily falter, go astray, and issue in disaster and the death of community.

In our time community has to be rebuilt from within. There have been changes in social structures and in social values which leave stable personality and community without their former supports, and the consequence has been disturbance and loss of direction both at the personal and the community level. But it is not possible to reach out and suddenly change the entire social structure around us or the social values which are the air we breathe. Structures and values change slowly, and only when people want them to change, even though desires and their fulfillment are often affected by historical and cultural factors beyond conscious control. In this sense, communities both initiate cultural changes and at the same time merely reflect deep-seated changing forces in cultural systems. Communities and their processes are in perpetual flux. The challenge is to do everything possible both to initiate social change and to direct the social current.

This fluidity in all of life is at once the source of our hope and the stimulus of our endeavors. We must first, with abundant hope, make those efforts which ensure our survival; then, going on from there, we must build from within more stable personalities and a more human community, even while we keep ourselves open to analyzing and promoting everything which can create a better environment. Enriched and stabilized, the human community we bring into being can act as a leaven, spreading its influence far beyond its own borders, as the great monastic communities did in the Dark Ages, assisting substantially in the building of the society which flowered in the high Middle Ages.

History is always repeating itself in its essential cycles, however different the accidental forms, because human nature remains basically the same. Nevertheless the accidental changes are often very real; sometimes they are of deep significance, affecting the essential ideals that direct men's lives. We must therefore cultivate a vital openness and the spirit of adaptation, remaining always ready to make whatever adjustments are needed if we are to be realistically in contact with life and with the real and felt needs of our fellow men. We must be neither immured in the past nor given over to abstract dreams of an ideal future.

Participation must always be our vital mystique. We must

contribute of our selves if we are to assist the ongoing process of organic growth in sociey, starting with the living and essential elements which come to us from the past. We must help to shape the basic directions of life both in accordance with the needs of the present and in accordance with those of the future, insofar as we can foresee them. But we may never pretend to write the laws of the universe for the next generation, even though we must try to leave them the best legacy we can.

But now for this question of community: perhaps we should first say what it is not. And I think we may safely say that place or space are not the essential elements. People can live in the same family, the same neighborhood, the same religious community, day after day, without communicating anything of their inner selves—without establishing the essential bonds on which community depends. Such a community is one in name only, or perhaps in legal status: it is not one in human or Christian functioning. Each member remains an island; there is no in-depth meeting of real persons.

Having defined the inner essence of community, we can now turn to its various definitions. First, we may say that a community can be either a structure or a process or both.

As structure, a community is any consciously organized grouping of individuals, residing, generally, in a specific area or locality, endowed with limited autonomy and recognizing certain degrees of unity and interdependence. According to their structured purpose, communities are matrimonial, familial, neighborhood, occupational, commercial, religious, and so on.

As a process, in the definition of the social scientists, a community is a society with positive aspects of social interaction. More descriptively, it includes all forms of association in which wasteful conflict has been reduced to a minimum and interpersonal relations aid human growth by fostering more intensive and more extensive attitudes and practices of interdependence, cooperation, and unification. A modern urban community progressively becomes a web of organized interest with very complex interactions.

Political scientists view community both as structure and process in which governmental forces arise from social interactions.

Social workers regard community as a grouping of families and as a system of institutions designed to exercise social control and assume social responsibilities. Modern urban life tends to functional and occupational groups rather than to neighborhood associations. An exception to this is in Japan, where such neighborhood groups have a centuries long tradition of action that embraces all vital intersts. Also in countries that are rapidly industrializing, such as Latin America, with a consequent mass movement of people from country to city, neighborhood associations are forming extensively in order to welcome, unite, and aid people in their struggle for identity and integration in a new way of life.

The personal status of the individual in modern communities derives from his relationship to a functional group. His personality and interests are likely to be best served by integration in organized groups that represent him. The unassociated individual suffers a greater or lesser loss both in status and in effective functioning.

Then there is the question of size: how big can a community be? It depends on its scope and on the level at which it functions. We have seen that the marriage of two persons is a community. At the other extreme, a political community can be vast, since its scope and the level of its communication are limited and mass means of communication are extensive. But unless a given community is capable of affording the individual a strong sense of self-identity and self-realization, resentment sets in against the depersonalization of the individual, or the departmentalization of personality, which results. This tends to be the experience of large organizations of any sort—governmental, commercial, or cultural. The individual rebels against the "establishment" because he feels unknown, unidentified as an individual, unattended in his personal needs and with little opportunity for personal expression. Hence the "participation mystique" which fires so many individuals, particularly among the young. To some extent—but only within limits—the intensive use of communication at every level can be made to compensate for the size of the community.

If we distinguish communities according to the scope and

the level of their communication, then the broadest and most all-embracing of communities is that whose bond is constituted by our common human nature. We may define human community as a society of persons who live—consciously or unconsciously—the commandments of God and are united by a common purpose deriving from their shared humanity, by an affective bond that includes a sense of belonging, and finally by regular communication which emphasizes mutual participation. Whether this is wholly possible of realization or not, this is the community projected by the structural unity of the race.

"Living the commandments" is a descriptive element of considerable meaning because the commandments are not something imposed from without to the detriment of personality but are simply the outward expression in positive form of that which our very nature requires for its protection and development. Therefore, if they are lived in the highest degree of fullness which can be expected of fallible human beings, they make for reasonably balanced personality.

Essentially, if a community is to be called human, the members must, with reasonable consistency, treat one another like human beings—that is, with a consideration and decency which avoids unnecessary threats, gives a maximum of understanding, compassion, and affective support, and provides an atmosphere of openness and encouragement to communication. There must be tolerance of differences and forgiveness of injuries; for otherwise hostility works as a corrosive in the individual personality and spreads into the community. There must be respect for the unique, creative capacity of each individual and a corporate responsibility for the development of each person.

Thinking realistically of the limits of man's nature in the human community, we may ask, "To what extent can a group be united?" To begin with, it is not to be expected that there should be complete intellectual agreement. A hundred factors of temperament, family background, experience, study, and feeling will make for disagreement. To some extent we must expect and want certain differences of opinion and approach so that each may, first of all, simply be precisely and distinctively that unique person whom God had in mind from all eternity and without whom God's order of being is not complete. Secondly, through diversity each can manifest a particular aspect of truth which God wishes to speak precisely through the special person he made each one to be, and which will stimulate the thinking and shape the decisions of the others. No one has a monopoly on truth. Each contributes a distinct aspect of the one truth; and the whole truth is not complete without the communication of each member. Thirdly, along with diversity of ideas and opinions there can be a unity of purpose, a conformity of free wills, an affective bond; a meeting of hearts.

And if it is a question of action to be taken, then unity can be achieved through majority vote. The minority in that case, and each person in the minority, by antecedent intelligent free choice recognizes the fact that action must be taken in spite of the inevitable differences of opinion and desire, and that the majority also are worthy of respect and have come to a judgment that, presumably, is best for the group. The majority, of course, can be wrong. But dialogue presupposes continued communication and adjustment in which errors are admitted and rectified. Finally, we must allow for the possibility of a rare genius who sees far beyond his contemporaries and, as a result, has to suffer misunderstandings and frustrations. But even for him, true dialogue permits the best chance to get a hearing and communicate truth.

What does "communication" mean in a human community? Obviously, it has to be more than mere monologue. A lecture or sermon or occasional talk, however, is not necessarily a monologue, for there can and should be a conscious meeting of the mind of the speaker with the needs of the listener, which establishes excellent communication. Ordinarily, communication is a true interchange of what all parties involved really think and feel. It cannot be a passive listening without response or participation, even though in the beginning of dialogue, whether casual or structured, it is understandable that those who are timid may be afraid to risk the expression of their opinions, the revelation of their true selves. Only gradually, reassured by being accepted as persons and by the atmosphere of tolerance which allays the fear they might have of making mistakes, will they begin to open up. Everyone in the group must bring this human understanding to the consideration of others' views. True communication requires active listening—that is, a true yielding of the mind and heart to what another person thinks and feels, so that the listener is able to understand why the speaker thinks and feels it and to state the speaker's position fairly and accurately.

Now that we have reviewed the definitions of community and seen its bearing on the development and fulfillment of the human person, the task remains of relating these data to the experience of God as it is found in the religious structures of our time. In their *Theological Dictionary* Karl Rahner and Herbert Vorgrimler explain how salvation history rests on the nature and the history of the race:

> From a philosophical point of view community is natural to Man, who can only arrive at his unique self by experiencing existence shared with other bodily, spiritual persons. Since fulfillment of the "I" can only occur through and in community, self-discovery and union with community grow in the same, not inverse, proportion. Theology explains and interprets man's nature as a social being in more detail; man is always the partner whom God himself has chosen, in such a way that he must realize his personal uniqueness *in* the community of all men and *in its service*. Thus God's self-communication to all men in Christ has not created a series of private saving histories for atomized individuals, but the *one* history of the *one* human race. Yet this history keeps each individual in view for his own sake; but he finds his way to himself—to himself as the person God has in view—only by finding that saving community which God himself has set up and personally realizing his membership of it.[1]

Earlier in this chapter we observed how God in his wisdom had presented his revelation to men in terms of the structures of which men have concrete experience: the family, the community. According to the same principle, the ecclesial structures through which the saving history of man is lived out must conform to the realities of his social nature. Without a truly human community there can be no Christian or parish or liturgical or religious community.

The Christian community is a unified society whose members, sealed with the Christ-seal and enlivened by his shared divine life, authentically live not only the commandments of God but also, and especially, the baptismal commitment to Christ and to his redeeming mission to teach, to govern, and to sanctify. Every Christian is therefore inescapably committed to suffer, in denial of self, all that is needed to redeem his community. He lives his life in a community of forgiven sinners. As a member of this community he should have at least a basic understanding of Christianity in its fullness and a sincere desire to live the Christ-life.

Within the Christian community the one Christ-life is lived out in various ways. A parish community is a fellowship of believers centered in corporate worship and family life, mutual support towards common ideals, human and spiritual growth. Its structure is determined partly by church organization and partly by the specific needs of pastor and people. The modern urban parish will need considerable adjustment to counteract the impersonality of urban industrial life so that it can really function as a true community. What changes will be needed to achieve its purpose are not altogether clear. But at least we may safely say that a Christian parish community can hardly be built where there is no natural human community.

> The secret of establishing a parish community is, first, to find out what are the natural communities which exist within the territory of the parish and then to bring the parish to each of these natural communities, while at the same time providing through the parish a structure in which the various natural communities can relate to one another.[2]

There will have to be some decentralizing of worship and spiritual service, the whole process orientated at once vertically to God and horizontally to the needs and desires of the people. Such a parish will minister to a necessity which is deeply human as well as spiritual; it will serve as a channel of love, encouraging and reinforcing the values on which Christian community depends. This is an undertaking which will call for much effort and sacrifice and especially for the self-denial involved in putting aside our masks and being sincerely the persons we are in community interaction with others.

It is a natural transition, given the desire for and commitment to community, to define our participation in the sacrificial union with Christ our Redeemer. The *liturgical or cultic community* is a fellowship of believers who through visible forms of worship corporately express their invisible union with God and with each other in him and reenact the continuing redemption of Christ. In the liturgy it is always Christ who is acting; and in each Mass and sacrament he uses his members to carry through a separate act of redemption. In an extended sense of the word, every Mass and all sacraments are a concelebration of all participating Christians. And quite literally, the Mass for the participating priests, confession for penitent and priest, and marriage for bride and groom are a redeeming concelebration.

But God needs a dedicated militia for special purposes, and he gives them a special grace to live a common life. A *religious community* is a unified Christian society whose members are dedicated not only to total human living by keeping God's commandments and their baptismal commitment to Christ and his mission, but also, according to the specific form and purpose of their own constitutions, to the living of the counsels of perfection. According to the needs of the time, they are engaged in an active apostolate as part of the Church's service to the world.

Finally, the *contemplative community* is a unified Christian society whose members are dedicated not only to living the commandments of God, the Christ-life, and their baptismal commitment to Christ and his mission, but also, according to the specific form of their constitutions, to living the counsels of perfection by centering their lives on disposing themselves for a deep union with God through prayer and penance.

The foregoing is, of course, only a sketch of the ecclesial structures of the Christian community. Their foundations lie deep in the past, and in a democratic age they still retain many traces of a monarchic way of governing. The whole question of authority, a key issue in our time, will be treated elsewhere. Here we have undertaken only to analyze the nature of community, particularly in relation to the saving community from which, as a center, the Christ-life issues, to work as a leaven in the wider society.

[1] New York: Herder and Herder, 1965, p. 91.
[2] Andrew Greeley, *The Hesitant Pilgrim* (New York: Sheed and Ward, 1966), p. 218.

CHAPTER 2

Social Factors Which Influence
the Experience of God in Community

Our world is no longer the closed world of the Old Testament, which, in spite of itself, was constantly being breached by social and commercial contacts, by wars and exiles. Nor is our world view that of the Middle Ages, limited by ignorance of the geographical extent of the universe and the variety of the cultures of mankind. Whatever point we specify as the beginning of the modern age, we must see the modern era as marked by expansion and by change. In our time the process of change has been accelerated to a degree formerly unknown, and there is every indication that change will become a permanent feature of life. At the same time, the growth of knowledge of the material universe is constantly increasing and constantly undergoing reversals because the data alter even as we study them.

All this renders the problem of applying eternal and absolute truths to modern society more difficult, especially since our standards of measurement are human and therefore fallible. Yet it is an undertaking which may not be abandoned, for Christianity is committed to the redemption of the world; and because Christian truths and principles may not be identified with any one culture nor any one moment of history, our undertaking involves detaching them from the outmoded thought forms of the past.

In the concrete we know that some things *ought* to be, and some *ought not* to be but *are*; and therefore, in this limited sense, they *must* be. Our Lord was a realist. "The poor you will always have with you," he said (Mt 26:11). "It is inevitable that scandal should occur" (Mt 18:7). "Did not the Messiah have to undergo all things so as to enter into his glory?" (Lk 24:26). Given the inescapable nature of these things which "must" be, there is a sense in which Christians always—and not just in our modern era with its variety of denominations—live and work in a pluralist society. For if Christianity is authentic, if it is practiced, it is almost everywhere and at all times the creed of a minority; inevitably it must be in contradiction to the things which ought not to be but are.

Christ accepted the naturally good things of life quite simply, but he never ceased his opposition to "the world" whose prince Satan is. The Beatitudes take into account the mingling of good and evil in the world; in them the things which, mysteriously, "must" be, owing to human guilt, remain somehow within God's plan. Evil and guilt are not willed by God, but they are known and used even in advance in the working out of the divine action in the world.

Hence from the Christian standpoint we no longer speak of social justice on a purely philosophical level but rather of a theology of liberation for a redeemed world in which God has become incarnate and man has an eternal destiny conformable to his spiritual nature. "There are not two histories, one profane and one sacred, juxtaposed or interrelated, but a single human progress, irreversibly exalted by Christ, the Lord of History. His redemptive work embraces every dimension of human existence."[1] Moreover, the eschatological dimension of the Christian promises implies that we have the power to change unjust social structures. "To fight for a just world, where there will be no oppression or slavery or forced work, will be a sign of the coming of the kingdom. Peace supposes the etablishment of justice (Is 32:17), defence of the rights of the poor, punishment of the oppressor, a life without fear of being enslaved."[2]

The fact that we unavoidably live in a society in which Christianity remains a contradiction to the defects of an environment which is largely secularist[3] has one particular consequence in our time: for it is evident that Church and State intersect in the individual conscience and that the proper functioning of both depends largely on the will of the individual. More than ever in this tolerant and permissive society the experience of God and moral conduct have to be a free and enlightened personal choice. And sincerity becomes a prime virtue. In the formation of the personal conscience ample guidelines from the past will enter, but without too many impositions of formal authority.

Parallel to this new emphasis on the individual conscience there has been a movement away from the concept of the clergy as a privileged upper class and an expansion of the role of the laity. And for clergy and laity as well, the necessity has developed of depending mainly on the authority of merit—that is, of competence and spiritual depth. Today everything that is said and written in religious matters must be carefully reasoned out and documented from life, without dependence on the citation of authority. This is true partly because authority itself is on a broader base and there is greater advertence to the dignity of the individual, and partly because Christians have become more conscious of the duty of bearing witness: there is always a non-Christian listening or reading.

This existential realism might constitute a danger if it were not kept within the context of a view in depth of man's spiritual dignity. The book of Genesis reveals in figurative language that the creation, including man and his salvation history, was originally conceived by God as a unity in which each thing is related to everything else in a mutual interdependence—not merely in the sense that all things are interconnected through being from the same origin, but in the sense that they are in communion with each other, all involved in the salvation history of man. Man's spiritual soul expresses itself, fulfills itself, through the body and through the penetration of material reality. Hence man cannot fulfill his spiritual and supernatural destiny except by infusing the spiritual into the material. This is the giant task of the Chrisitan in the secularist world.

Natural creation, the communication of God's being and

his power, is ordered to redemption, which is the self-communication of God incarnate. Through the passion, death, and resurrection of God-made-man redemption is in principle achieved; but its fulfillment in time is the task of men living with the risen life of Christ.

This ordering of the creation to redemption lays the whole material universe open to salvation history and gives everything an ultimately supernatural meaning. It also confirms creation in its true and permanent naturalness and seeks to heal the wounds it has suffered as the consequence of man's sin. This means that every natural created entity is ordered to grace in such a way that it cannot remain really whole and sound in itself, nor achieve the completion required by its own nature, unless it is integrated into the supernatural order of grace.

God did not create two realities which needed subsequently to be harmonized; the opposition which man experiences from the forces of nature comes from the fact that sin entered the world. Nevertheless man is not born to conflict but to the conquest of unity in the divine order of creation. This unity, from the standpoint of eternity already achieved, is in history still unfulfilled, vulnerable, hidden. Man is charged with the responsibility of achieving unity within himself and in his environment and of manifesting in the creation the unity hidden in the redemptive order.

There are in general two wrong directions which the human effort towards fulfillment can take. At one extreme there is a pessimism which turns away from the world, seeing it as radically disordered and wholly hostile. At the other there is an excess of optimism which takes the form of utopianism. Both are false orientations towards the world. The pessimist fails to see that the world, despite the evils in it, remains Christ's; therefore, discounting the power of Christ at work in society, he tends to withdraw from responsibility and from collaboration with others. The utopian, on the other hand, overrating the possibilities of this world for developing the capacities of man and bringing him fulfillment, is forgetful of his supernatural vocation. Oblivious of the fact that all our human undertakings have their term in the world to come, he tries prematurely and violently to impose a consummation in his own time, not waiting for Christ's coming. Thus the natural order which has been redeemed suffers disruption; natural forces which should mature slowly to reach their fullness are hindered by the pressure of haste, the rhythm of nature is disturbed. Above all, human personality suffers. We see the effect of this in all the undertakings in society which fail to take the spiritual dimension into account, but most especially in the tragic frustrations of the totalitarianisms, where so many thousands are still imprisoned or subject to the rule of a police state more than half a century after the "first" stage in the achievement of utopia was supposed to have begun.

Indeed, the divine action in the world is hidden from our experience and can only be known by faith; only by faith can we be certain that God remains in control. The "profane" world —that is, the world seen purely in its secularity—is opaque, almost totally impenetrable. Its harsh inhumanities seem inevitable. The unfinished unity conceals itself, partly because it has its roots in grace, which works anonymously in and through nature, and partly because it is being achieved through the scandal of the cross.

But now, to turn to the factors in our society which are inimical to the development of community and thus hinder the mission of community to restore the divine unity in the world: we shall have to concern ourselves first with matters of sociology. We shall have, in the present context, to consider these factors in a negative way, but we shall try to avoid overextension and oversimplification. We do not pretend to have all the answers.

It is obvious that the mobility of modern society is a hindrance to community: never before have so many people moved from place to place in their lifetimes. What each move means, of course, is the wrench of breaking away from neighborhood ties with all the bonds of affection and responsibility which they involve. Often, in the new neighborhood, the associations which are formed have less depth; and when moves are frequent, stable contacts tend to decline. The result is frequently a decline in the sense of responsibility for the neighbor; people feel increasingly "free" to go their own way and leave others free to go theirs—free, too, to look after themselves.

Even more serious is the fact that the shifting of locale usually brings with it a tendency to shift values to the prevailing winds of the environment. Hence there is a lack of the permanent ethical moorings which are so necessary for community life and the experience of God.

Another characteristic of our society, which is equally obvious, is that it is highly mechanistic without ceasing to be humanistic. The combination has been productive of benefits unknown in the past; yet we are not always sure how much the human is given its due part nor how much the mechanistic may be damaging the human person. In any case, we move in a world of industry, of industries which manufacture and industries which package, distribute and serve. The machines and gadgets continue to multiply and become increasingly important, even dominant, in the lives of most people. Hence the panic when the wheels of industry seem to be slowing down in a recession—or when electrical power fails for a few hours. But striking the balance between the good and the harmful depends not only on the counting of material benefits but also on a full consideration of man's total human nature and destiny, and of the toll taken of his psychic energy, which by right should belong to the experience of God.

Without question, technology has conferred real benefits in making our culture more humane. The powerful social forces which limit the work week have gathered strength from the wider distribution of wealth in modern society and have been a healthy reaction against the domination of the machine. We can applaud when industry becomes the patron of education, the arts, and social welfare projects, for then it is already doing something to redress the balance of the harm done by a world of machines. Nevertheless we must not ignore the fact that industry is not free of the tendency to consider the operator as part of the machine and to enforce a machinelike standard of production as the condition of survival in the job. There are, of course, a variety of factors involved in the phenomenon of able-bodied people resorting to the dole and it would be invalid to over-emphasize the role of technology. However, would it be wholly unreasonable to suppose that the pressure for high production to which the individual worker is subjected might be a factor in rebellion against all forms of "being forced"? Might not the impersonality of such working conditions (in which too often no account is taken of the quality of the individual's work) con-tribute mightily to the boredom and frustration which lead work-ers into excesses with respect to sex, alcohol, and drugs, or even explode into violence?

Another trait of our culture which is self-evident is that it is highly pragmatic. "Does it work?" is the question raised with regard to practically everything. Now "Does it work?" is a good question, but it is not the only question. Equally important are the questions "To what purpose does it work?" and "With what results for all concerned does it work?" Yet these latter are often not asked at all. Too often there is an unquestioning preoccupa-tion with production, results, and—above all—success. These are, of course, legitimate objectives, and to be motivated by the desire for them is good when it is kept within rational limits. But success is generally conceived as surpassing others, and therefore it involves a consuming concern with what others think and a tendency towards conformity for the sake of acceptance. Even worse, it sometimes involves the use of other people for one's own objectives, who are discarded when these objectives are attained. Where does God enter in here?

So deeply entrenched is this pragmatic approach to life that it has invaded the sphere of self-realization, often subtly and mixed with a certain amount of real idealism. In community, this generates an attitude of "What does the community do for me, personally?" "How will commitments work out for me? Will they transform me and solve my personal problems?" Or, put in another way, "Do commitments 'work' in our time, in the sense that their witness is recognized?" Inevitably, then, when the question of whether things "work" is identified with immediate results, the emphasis is on the tangible and concrete at the natural level of personality fulfillment and on possessing things and using them freely. With this emphasis on *doing* and *producing*, channeled into our involvements with the world and other people, there is a consequent deemphasis on *being*, and particularly on being with God in prayer, presumably because these aspects of life seem to have less relevance.

Too often the result is an alienation from the deepest level of self and from God. Then "self-realization" is orientated towards the purely secular values, and the criteria of "situation ethics" leave the divine law out of account. It is not surprising that there should be, on the other hand, those who do not "adjust" but react with nonconformity or rebellion, rejecting goals so unworthy of the sublime destiny of man; or, again, those who are rendered purposeless by boredom.

Another factor militating against community is the *impersonality* of our society. This is most marked in the larger cities, where we all become accustomed to ignoring thousands of people since that seems the only way to survive. So often the dwellers in the highrise apartment buildings do not know their next-door neighbors, to say nothing of the people on the next street. But apart from residential considerations, we have fallen into the habit of thinking of people as objects—in terms of social problems, first of all, but there are other categories: the patient, the worker, the customer, the voter, the ball player, the artist, and so on. Too often the value placed upon the person is attached to the role he plays, and the person himself is lost in the statistics belonging to the category.

This impersonality is increased by the intricate network of institutions, organizations, and enterprises which strongly affect everyone in one way or another. And the more governmental bureaucracy expands, the more impersonal it becomes. Institution and industry make considerable efforts to reduce this impersonality through the employment of public relations experts, counselors, psychiatrists for the assistance of personnel, and the efforts are praiseworthy when their motives are good. But they are rarely productive of the intimate person-to-person relationships which condition us for the experience of God.

We live in a culture which has developed a high degree of *secularity*,[4] and the trend is on the increase. So far as religion is concerned, it is not so much a question of withdrawal from the churches as it is one of keeping God, the one divine reality, out of the center of life. What is in question is not so much his existence as his relevance. Whether this attitude is verbalized or not, the fact is that in our society God has to a great extent ceased to be Someone with whom men enter into a personal relationship. As a consequence comes the other question, "Is a definite creed or practice important?" Modern man has reverted to the primitive way of making a god in his own image and likeness, and in his worship therefore he often finds no one but himself. With God relegated to the periphery of life in an area vaguely thought of as "spiritual" man tries, on the one hand, to absolutize a variety of other values—power, success, sex, the certitude of scientific knowledge. On the other hand, he tries to make an evil of everything that is opposed to his "god" of the moment. Thus objective standards of truth and goodness lose their stability, and there is a decline in the authority of the norms on which our culture rests.

Finally, there is a *disintegration of family life* in our time. The reasons are complex, but it is evident that both men and women are experiencing increasing difficulty in defining their roles in marriage. The result for the children is an impoverishment of that first community in which they should learn how to be secure in their self-identity and how to relate to others, beginning with their parents. Thus, when their early needs for socialization are not met, they find it difficult to form strong and lasting relationships in the adult society into which they emerge. Deprived of the father image which normally prepares for the experience of God, children often acquire resentments which they transfer from their fathers to any male authority—or, if it is the mother who is resented, to any female authority.

Even where married people have succeeded, against such great odds as are found in the contemporary world, in creating a stable home, they will find it difficult to preserve that home as a community in the face of the distractions of the mass media, which today invade the home like a third line of authority, exerting an influence running counter to the values parents are striving to inculcate.

Everywhere we look we see evidence that all our traditional institutions are being tested by our youth: the family, the university, the church, our democratic form of government—all are the objects of rebellion and, at the extreme, of rejection. And yet the scene is not entirely dark, for nonconformism is not necessarily unhealthy. Indeed, when a society seems to have lost its direction, the contrary is the case. And so, having faced the negative aspects realistically, we find many solid reasons for hope. In many fine and capable young people who have broken out of the pattern of life which the older generation would impose on them we see the quest for self-identity bearing wholesome fruit in a shift away from irresponsible freedom to a responsible dedication to helping the underprivileged. This represents a healthy movement away from abstract ideals towards truth and reality found in people as they are in their existential needs. It calls for courage in facing the inevitable risks of such work and faith in the basic goodness and reasonableness of our fellow men. And since it begins with each person doing what he personally feels is needed, out of a sense of the bond which binds him to others, it means the restoration of the person and a new beginning of community.

Today it is in the small-scale enterprises of a responsible minority, which says of the things which *ought* to be in our society, "Why not?" that civilization is renewing itself. For these undertakings, so broadly human in their purposes, are capable of engaging a great diversity of human personalities in one corporately functioning community. The realization of these visions will inevitably call for much dialogue, and with it will come the bonds which arise from mutual respect and trust. In the end the barriers of race and class which have resisted direct, large-scale political action will yield to the reality of true community.

It will take time, of course, for the small-scale enterprise to have large issue. And yet, wherever it is initiated a beginning is made of renewing the divine action of redeeming the world and the unity of all creation begins to shine through again. Where love is, God is. "As the mystics felt instinctively," writes Teilhard de Chardin, "everything becomes physically and literally lovable in God; and God, in return, becomes intelligible and lovable in everything around us."[5]

[1] Gustavo Gutiérrez, "Notes for a Theology of Liberation," *Theological Studies* 31 (June 1970), p. 255.

[2] Ibid., p. 256.

[3] Cf. below, ch. 23.

[4] The relation of the secular to the sacred will receive special treatment in our final chapter.

[5] *Science and Christ* (New York: Harper and Row, 1969).

CHAPTER 3

The Value of the Human Person

In a rapidly changing environment the only thing outside God that remains stable is the human person. This is at once our despair and our hope: our despair because man's past history is marked by so many tragic errors, weighed down by such a burden of evil; our hope because this history is also a record of a struggle upwards towards the mastery of his environment, towards the creation of a civilization which manifests his immense capacity for good. Edmund Burke said, "The one thing necessary for the triumph of evil is that good men do nothing"; but evil does not triumph, though it may sometimes seem to. We have only to think of how, when some natural disaster strikes, the men who yesterday seemed indifferent to the lot of the less fortunate fly to the rescue with tremendous quantities of food, clothing, and financial help. But apart from such extra-ordinary events there is in general in our society, side by side with its competitive ethic, an intense concern to improve social conditions with respect to housing, nutrition, medical services, educational and employment opportunities and the like.

Unfortunately it is true, of course, that there are some who have lost the meaning of the human person because they do not admit the truth concerning man's origin and his eternal destiny. For the atheist human life is cheap. One recalls that Voltaire forbade his friends to ridicule God in the presence of his servants. "If my servants do not believe in God, there is no reason why they should not murder me in my bed." Western society has come a long way from this cynical practicality.

"There is a growing awareness of the exalted dignity proper to the human person," wrote Pope John, "since he stands above all things, and his rights and duties are universal and inviolable. Therefore, there must be available to all men everything necessary for leading a life truly human, such as . . . the right . . . to a good reputation, to respect . . . to activity in accordance with the upright norm of one's own conscience, to protection of privacy and to rightful freedom in matters religious too" (*Pacem in Terris*, no. 12).

Our hope, as we have said, is in the extent to which modern man is a man of good will. Yet with all the immense development of science and technology which multiplies more and more both the instruments of work and the comforts of a life full of opportunities for leisure and recreation, why is there increasingly greater restlessness, loneliness, alienation, aimlessness in our society? Why do so many lives lose direction and erupt into violence? Can it be that modern man lacks the prudence which would enable him to employ the skills of his civilization in ways which contribute to his self-fulfillment as man? Can it be that he lacks this basic prudence because he has pushed God out of his life, thinking of him as belonging to the sphere of "religion"—instead of being at the center of all reality?

It is part of man's value as a person that he is not merely the recipient of creation but is its agent as well. What we make happen as co-creators with God can be just as much the will of God as what happens independently of our action. Our formation of ourselves as persons involves making ourselves appropriate instruments of God, partners with God, forming things and other persons in accordance with his will and his purposes for them. Hence the meaning of prudence. "Prudence," says Augustine, "is love discerning correctly that which helps us and that which hinders us in our going to God."

The changes that are taking place in the world today affect everyone, including those we love. No one of us is free to remain indifferent to the crises of our civilization; we must all respond with the best we have. But before we can serve as co-creators with God we must come to an understanding of what man is.

Man is a mystery. He is capable of the uttermost degradation and the uttermost heroism. He is dwarfed by the immensity of the universe which science has revealed; yet the science is man's own knowledge. Whether walking behind a plough or walking in space, he represents a force superior to the material universe which seems to dwarf him.

We can make some beginning at the measurement of man's mystery by the following criteria concerning his nature: (1) his natural capacities, which make him capable of great error and evil and of nobility and sanctity as well; (2) the immensity of his achievements in every sphere; (3) the capacity and need whereby one person is complemented by another; and (4) the capacity and need of the human person for communicating with divinity. Of the first two we have already spoken; we shall concern ourselves for the rest of this chapter with the third and fourth.

Man is made to share his substance with other men, to reach out towards them and enrich their lives. It is a law very deep in his being. Far from exhausting his resources by pouring out his being, it is only by this means that he achieves his own growth and maturity. The more he is disposed to give himself, the more he deepens his own resources and enlarges his capacity for serving others. Indeed if a man fails to follow this law of his nature, he will lose the resources which should be his through failing to develop them.

Unless we are able to open ourselves to other persons, no material thing or achievement will assist the inner development which is essential to our happiness. So profound and rich is the nature of human personality that only the sharing of the wealth of another human person can complement it. The wisdom of the ages has recognized this: ''A faithful friend is beyond price, no sum can balance his worth'' (Sir 6:14-15). The value of a friend is much more than that of physical shelter: he is another self with whom it is possible to share the sacred depths of one's being. Without someone with whom he can relate, a man cannot communicate his thoughts, his plans and hopes, his love. Only another human person can understand his thoughts, share his feelings, clarify his intentions, counsel and support him in his hopes and his needs.

This need for another is very complex because the person that each one is embraces the past, the present, and the future. A man wants to communicate something of the persons and experiences of the past which have formed him, something of what is happening within him and in his environment in the present, and something of himself which he has already projected into the future through his plans and his hopes. Without this possibility of intercommunication men remain frustrated, incomplete, and unfulfilled. It is above all through friendship in marriage that the interchange between two persons reaches its most profound, most intimate, most enriching, and most satisfying expression.

This relatedness to others finds another real, though less direct, expression in those persons who have experienced something so deeply that they feel an intense need to pour it out in writing and the other arts. Or they may express themselves in a scientific way through construction, laboratory research, agriculture, or the exploration of space. Mothers and fathers express their creativeness in the rearing of the children they bring into the world, each a unique creation; in the love which makes their house a home. Indeed, men cannot contain within themselves their fullness of life, the creative wealth of their nature. It must overflow into the service of other men in order to reach its meaning and purpose.

The way towards self-realization is through many conquests. We must conquer the fears and self-deceptions which close us in upon ourselves. We must take the risks of friendship with our fellow men, because each risk is a sign of love and an invitation to the deepening of intercommunication. We must learn to confide in others and to receive their confidences, to sympathize and rejoice with them. In a word, we have to love by giving ourselves to others. Only by interesting ourselves in all of life and being ready to commit ourselves deeply shall we fully realize ourselves.

However, no matter what a man can be or accomplish at

the natural level, either alone or with others, he has only begun to tap his potentialities. For in the final analysis, he can be measured only in terms of the infinite, the divine.

The Scriptures help us to evaluate man; they hold up the mirror to him and invite him to look into the depths of his own being. Little by little we are coming to an understanding of the psychological depths of the Bible. There is much in the laws of Moses that parallels the laws of other ancient peoples (and indeed in part actually springs from them). The really distinctive thing about the Mosaic Law, something never found among pagans, was the intuition about the dignity of each human person. What would account for this difference between cultures belonging to the same ancient world?

The answer must be found in the covenant relationship between God and his people Israel. To this people God revealed himself not only in his majesty and omnipotence but also in his tenderness and mercy as a Father. He entered into a familiar and affectionate relationship with them which took the concrete form of a contract whereby he manifested his respect for their capacity to receive very special privileges and to exercise responsibility by carrying out special obligations.

From this solemn contract with the Most High God flowed a sense of social justice. There were laws for the protection of widows and the poor, for securing the rights of property and of inheritance. But apart from law, there was the obligation which each individual felt towards the community because the Israelite community was the chosen people of God.

Insofar as the protection promised by the covenant with God depended upon the fidelity of Israel in carrying out its own side of the contract, Israel made its own history, suffering defeat and disgrace in its unfaithfulness and enjoying victory and the divine blessing in its repentance. And thus Israel's progress in the knowledge of God moved forward.

At about the year 750 B.C., through the prophet Hosea, the relation between God and his people became deeper and more personal when God compared it to the love of friendship between husband and wife. This revelation of God's tenderness was at the same time a revelation of the sacredness of human love and of the fact that it was part of man's value as a person that he was created to know and to love.

Therefore little by little, as the Israelites advanced in the understanding of God's love, it became clear that the covenant, though imposed in legal form, was not a restriction inimical to life but a benevolent guide to making and carrying through a personal commitment that was total and profoundly free. God's commandments were seen for what they are—not something imposed from without which would diminish personal freedom but an external expression in positive form of that which our nature itself needs for its growth and fulfillment. At the same time this personal relationship between God and his chosen people, growing in intimacy, was serving as a preparation for God's final revelation, which was the coming of his Son, Jesus Christ.

The teaching of Christ further enriched our understanding of the value of man. In Christ, true God and true man, God brought to its fullness his revelation of himself and of man, made in his image and likeness. In Christ he became one of us, sharing in our life with all its trials, sufferings, and innocent joys. In Christ the natural man is raised to its highest dignity; when the Word is made flesh, a woman becomes the mother of God.

Central to Christ's teaching is the revelation of the Trinity. God is no solitary Supreme Being, no mere First Cause, as we should conceive him by unaided reason, but an Eternal Father who communicates himself. God the Father eternally generates a Son who receives the divine nature in its totality. Between the Father and the Son there is eternally an outpouring of love, a "breathing" through which the third Person, the Holy Spirit, receives the divine nature from the Father and the Son. Each of the Persons is the same God; yet they are not identical—the Son is not the Father, the Holy Spirit is not the Son. To use the strictly theological term, a Person in the Trinity is a subsistent relation: each is the same God, since he possesses the divine nature totally; and yet each is "another" by way of relation. For the Father eternally begets the Son; the Son is eternally begotten; the Holy Spirit eternally receives the divine nature from the Father and the Son.

The tri-personal inner life of God is a mystery which transcends human reason; we could learn of it only from God himself. Yet it is a mystery which becomes luminous when we consider our own human nature in the light it gives. From it we learn that relationship with another is the heart and indispensable necessity of personality. The divine trinitarian life from which all being takes its origin consists in an interpersonal exchange of knowledge and love. We are made in God's image and likeness, and so the more our life is lived relationally, in a community whose law is love, the more deeply we shall enter into the divine life which is the source of the whole creation.

CHAPTER 4

Our First Vocation
Is to Be Our Distinctive Selves

We happen only once. "Make the most of yourself," says Gerard Manley Hopkins, "for you will never happen again." The reason why each of us exists is the goodness of the infinite God diffusing itself. God did not create the world out of any necessity, but only out of love: he loved that idea of us which was in his divine intellect from all eternity. And in creating men God never repeats himself: he makes each of us utterly unique, distinct from anyone who has ever been, is now, or ever will be. In our uniqueness, the self which each one of us is, is steeped in mystery—ineffable. This self which we call our own is a gift from God; it is also an invitation to become fully what we are, to realize our true self in all its richness and depth. What we are reveals itself in life situations, and we are called to achieve self-identity. Our first vocation is to be ourselves.

Our vocation as Christians is full of hope: Christian realism is Christian optimism. We are twice-born, first of human stock and secondly, through our baptism, into the risen life of Christ. At baptism God reaches into the heart of our being and transforms it at its dynamic center, empowering us to live with the life of grace, in the supernatural order of faith, hope, and love. Through baptism we are incorporated into the body of Christ to become his members; baptized into Christ's death, we rise with Christ; becoming sons of God, we are the brothers and sisters of Christ, our eldest brother, the first-born of the dead. And as long as we are in God's friendship we are indwelt by the Father, the Son, and the Holy Spirit, taken up into the love between them. "If a man loves me," Christ said at the Last Supper, "he will keep my word, and my Father will love him, and we will come to him and make our home with him" (Jn 14:23). And so there is a sense in which, during our earthly pilgrimage, we already have heaven in our hearts. "All the way to heaven is heaven," says St. Catherine of Siena, "because he said, 'I am the way.'"

So closely are we united to Christ as members of his body that we can cry out in the conclusion to the Canon of the Mass: "Through him, with him, and in him, in union with the Holy Spirit, all honor and glory to the Father!" So radically altered are we by our incorporation into Christ that we can never think of ourselves again as merely natural persons, however magnificently endowed we may be by nature; for then we should be abstracting ourselves from the real person we really and mysteriously are in Christ: our baptism effects a permanent change which cannot be reversed. It is for ever. And yet grace works through nature, and we are immersed in nature; we fulfill our vocation to become fully what we are within the context of our historical condition.

While we must begin and end by situating ourselves in the fullness of our Christian being and embracing this fullness in everything we say and do, it is nevertheless vital to attain a true concept of what we are in our process of becoming. There are two opposite errors to be avoided: naturalism and angelism. Naturalism, by leaving out of account the radical change which took place when the supernatural life was engrafted into nature to work through it, would reduce our human life to a purely rational, emotional, and physical existence. It leads to self-doubt, even to self-hatred, until a person becomes unable to experience himself as lovable. Consequently, lacking any sense of being loved, he is unable to give love. He can neither understand nor live the command to love one's neighbor as oneself.

Angelism, on the other hand, would conceive of spirit as the only thing that matters. In this view the body, with all its physical, psychological, and emotional needs, is something to be merely tolerated.

But that is not the way God made us. Again we are making the mistake of abstracting ourselves from the real persons we are. We are not spirits embodied in the flesh as in a prison, we are incarnated persons. This being true, we establish the right relation between soul and body when we accept certain restraints and disciplines as part of normal Christian life. They do not destroy our humanness or diminish it, but rather make us more completely, more genuinely, human by bringing the instincts under the control of reason and will and restoring order to our complex constitution. They make the body a more responsive instrument of the faculties which most distinghish us from the animals, the mind and will. Thus we become more capable of returning to God his gifts both of the body and of the spirit.

As we said above, this self which each of us is, is steeped in mystery. It can be glimpsed and tasted in those moments of quiet when we are at peace within ourselves; when we have set aside, for the time being, the mask which we present to the outside world, the pretense, from which few of us are free, of being something other than what we are. This unique reality of self which we experience at such rare moments is the only reality with which God can work in molding us unto a closer likeness to himself.

In this life all our knowledge is by way of ideas. Thus, we have an idea of a thing—or, to put it in another way, a mental word which represents it. But the idea is not the thing itself; it is only the reflection of the thing in our mind. It is, in the last analysis, in this way that we know both ourselves and others, however close our association with them—imperfectly, obscurely, through a reflection in the mind. And these images which we have of ourselves and others are limited by all the imperfections which belong to our human condition and to us personally. We are unable to express the person we are; what the other person is in his intimate depths is hidden from us. Only God knows the person.

In very truth the only man in history in whom the person

has ever been totally expressed is Our Lord Jesus Christ, "the Son of his love, who is the image of the invisible God, born before all creatures" (Col 1:13,15). God's Word took our human nature to show his love for us, and if we have not in us the mind of Christ, then we shall not know ourselves or our fellow men even in the way which is possible in view of our human limitations.

First, as to our image of ourselves: we shall not see ourselves clearly unless we see ourselves as contingent beings dependent upon God from moment to moment for our very existence and for the only reality there is in anything we think, say, or do. But God has made it a tender, person-to-person dependence, a dependence in love. So we read in the Psalms:

> O Lord, my heart is not lifted up,
>   my eyes are not raised too high;
> I do not occupy myself with things
>   too great and too marvelous for me.
> But I have calmed and quieted my soul,
>   like a child quieted at his mother's breast;
>   like a child that is quieted is my soul.
> O Israel, hope in the Lord
>   from this time forth and for evermore.
>   (Ps 131:1-3, RSV)[1]

The inspired song of the psalmist is in a sense a mother's lullaby sung back to her by her child. The mother delights in the child's return of her tenderness: but, greater wonder still, the transcendent, omnipotent God is glorified by the return of love from his creatures. In our time the encyclical *Mystici Corporis* has presented us with an amazing insight—namely, that there is a sense in which God needs us. It is possible to say that he is dependent upon us to bring his eternal glory to its fullness by the completion of our own redemption. Christ needs his members, writes Pope Pius XII, not owing to any weakness of his own, but because he has *chosen* to need them.

In God there is no past or future, he sees everything in the eternal *now*; so also God sees every one of us in the present as the unique, irreplaceable person he made us to be. Hence it is possible for each one of us to say: "I alone can give God the unique adoration and love which he made me personally to give. Nobody else in the history of the world can give precisely that adoration, thanksgiving, and love, make precisely that reparation which is mine to give and to make." Others can make some reparation for our failure, but they cannot substitute for us. So there is a special mysterious sense in which St. Paul could say: "In my flesh I fill up what is lacking in the sufferings of Christ for the sake of his body, the Church" (Col 1:24). Each of us, his members, make up in our flesh, for his body which is the Church, that share of suffering which he requires of us personally.

Secondly, as to our image of others: we shall see them clearly only if we see them each as unique, irreplaceable, one loved by God. Other people are not targets at which we are to aim acts of virtue as if we were playing a game of darts. The Christian life is not a game of practicing acts of virtue, not a mechanical balancing of the books. We are to love the person in the obscurity which inevitably characterizes all of our knowledge of him, and our love must begin with reverence, a reverence which forbids any use of him merely for any purpose of our own.

However well we have learned to love in the personal relationships of this life, there is a secret citadel within our being to which only God can penetrate, a place in our hearts which only God can fill. This means that everyone, this side of heaven, whatever his vocation in life, is just a little bit lonely. God reserves for himself the unshared and unshareable core of our being, and so, during our earthly pilgrimage, we are lonely for him. It is his will that we should never be satisfied in this life but should long for the life to come in which we shall know even as we are known. Meanwhile we should live in expectation, and the note of thanksgiving should never be absent from our worship, the expression of our gratitude for the amazing gift of self:

> I give you thanks that I am fearfully,
>   wonderfully made; wonderful are your works.

> *My soul also you knew full well;*
> *nor was my frame unknown to you*
> *when I was made in secret.*
> *How weighty are your designs, O God;*
> *how vast the sum of them!*

(Ps 139:14-15,17)

[1] *RSV: The Holy Bible, Revised Standard Version* (New York: Nelson, 1953). Copyright 1946 and 1952 by the Division of Christian Education of the National Council of the Churches of Christ in the U.S.A.

CHAPTER 5

Freedom and Responsibility in Community

In our highly organized, complex civilization of the second half of the twentieth century, when man is thought to have come to maturity out of an unscientific past, great stress is placed on freedom, responsibility, and creative activity. Freedom, especially, is stressed in every sector of our culture, since without it responsibility and creative activity cannot develop.

The emancipation of modern man through the spirit of scientific inquiry has been fraught with immense consequences for both good and evil. On the one hand, man has achieved a conquest of nature unparalleled in the past; on the other, he has released forces which threaten to overwhelm his culture—and human life itself—unless he learns to bring them under control. It is in his creative activity that man exhibits most strikingly his likeness to God; in it he collaborates with God's continuing act of creation. But the very greatness of man's gifts contains perils. For example, the discovery of nuclear fission and of the atomic energy which it yields is potentially the source of immense benefits to man, but it also contains possibilities of hardly conceivable disaster. For it carries human freedom to a peak of power never before attained. From now on, man will always have to face the question of the ultimate use of freedom, the ultimate choice—wholly real in our time—as to whether he will destroy himself or survive. Insofar as we can take in the implications of so awesome an event, it seems clear that men can continue to exist on this planet only if they freely choose to do so, for they now have the power of self-annihilation.

One wonders whether Machiavelli could remain so cooly certain of the validity of his political principle of the balance of power in face of the alignment of intercontinental ballistic missiles ready to carry multi-megaton bombs capable of destroying whole countries. One wonders whether those great libertarians of the past—Rabelais or Rousseau, for instance—might not be given second thoughts about their unqualified advocacy of individual liberty? Never before in the history of the world has it been so vital that freedom should have its counterweight of responsibility.

Yet it is precisely responsibility which is undergoing great strains in the environment in which our generation finds itself after the catastrophes of two world wars. For the nearly incalculable destruction of war has been paralleled by moral disasters in the dubious peacetime, with its undeclared wars, which has followed. Everywhere we look we see a weakening and deterioration of family life, education, government, religious culture. The discipline which characterized earlier generations has on a large scale been replaced by the pleasure principle, and the result is that many of us tend to live half-lives, using only a part of our resources for self-development and the building up of our environment. (Rollo May, in his book *Love and Will*, elaborates the reasons for this.)

The Second Vatican Council, in its Pastoral Constitution on the Church in the Modern World (no. 5), took account of the forces in modern society which militate against the most urgent task which confronts the men of our era—that of humanizing the civilization which is the product of science and technology:

> Today's spiritual agitation and the changing conditions of life are part of a broader and deeper revolution. As a result of the latter, intellectual formation is ever increasingly based on the mathematical and natural sciences and on those dealing with man himself, while in the practical order the technology which stems from these sciences takes on mounting importance . . . .
>
> History itself speeds along on so rapid a course that an individual person can scarcely keep abreast of it. The destiny of the human

community has become all of a piece, where once the various groups
of men had a kind of private history of their own. Thus, the human
race has passed from a rather static concept of reality to a more
dynamic, evolutionary one. In consequence there has arisen a new
series of problems, a series as important as can be, calling for
new efforts of analysis and synthesis.

Speaking of the impact of these profound social changes on
religion and morality, the council goes on to say (no. 7):

A more critical ability to distinguish religion from a magical view
of the world and from the superstitions which still circulate, purifies
religion and exacts day by day a more personal and explicit adherence to faith. As a result many persons are achieving a more vivid
sense of God.

On the other hand, growing numbers of people are abandoning
religion in practice. Unlike former days, the denial of God or religion, or the abandonment of them, are no longer unusual and
individual occurrences. For today it is not rare for such decisions
to be presented as requirements of scientific progress or of a certain
new humanism. In numerous places these views are voiced not
only in the teachings of philosophers, but on every side they influence literature, the arts, the interpretation of the humanities and
of history, and civil laws themselves. As a consequence, many
people are shaken.

Commenting on the impact of drastic social change on the
individual, the council writes:

Within the individual person there too often develops an imbalance
between an intellect which is modern in practical matters, and
a system of thought which can neither master the sum total of
its ideas, nor arrange them adequately into a synthesis. Likewise,
an imbalance arises between the conditions of collective existence
and the requisites of personal thought, and even of contemplation.
Specialization in any human activity can at length deprive man
of a comprehensive view of reality. (Ibid., no. 8)

Our age, then, is one which presents enormous obstacles
to the development of the freedom to which man is called. Human
liberty is relative, not absolute; in part it is a gift from God
and in part it must be attained by the conquest of all those

forces within ourselves and in our environment which hinder it. Speaking of the problem of freedom as it presents itself to the Christian in our permissive society, the council says:

> Only in freedom can man direct himself toward goodness. Our contemporaries make much of this freedom and pursue it eagerly; and rightly so, to be sure. Often, however, they foster it perversely as a license for doing whatever pleases them, even if it is evil.
>
> For its part, authentic freedom is an exceptional sign of the divine image within man. For God has willed that man be left "in the hand of his own counsel" so that he can seek his Creator spontaneously, and come freely to utter and blissful perfection through loyalty to Him. Hence man's dignity demands that he act according to a knowing and free choice. Such a choice is personally motivated and prompted from within. It does not result from blind internal impulse nor from mere external pressure.
>
> Man achieves such dignity when, emancipating himself from all captivity to passion, he pursues his goal in a spontaneous choice of what is good, and procures for himself, through effective and skillful action, apt means to that end. Since man's freedom has been damaged by sin, only by the help of God's grace can he bring such a relationship with God into full flower. Before the judgment seat of God each man must render an account of his own life, whether he has done good or evil. (Ibid., no. 17)

The emancipation from captivity to passion of which the council speaks will be the issue of a lifetime struggle. There are two areas in particular where we can help ourselves by a growth in awareness.

First, to remain free from social and emotional pressures or to resist blind instincts seeking unlawful satisfaction, we need clear and solid principles. These principles provide the rational convictions which guide our decisions, either in crisis or in ordinary daily duties and occurrences. The principles have their greatest force when they are embodied in habits. What is known as character is a complex of habits derived from principles which flow into consistent action. Principles can result either from natural or supernatural motives. They must be worked out through discussion and open interchange with others, and draw upon all the available sources of truth.

Our human intelligence uses facts and principles to guide and control freedom. The intellect receives into itself, considers, and judges the data of experience in the light of principles both natural and supernatural and within the perspective of past, present, and future. Normally the intellect keeps us free from error in matters which are within its province, but with regard to questions having a moral dimension we need the help of grace.

Second, in our exercise of freedom, emotions can either help or hinder us, and it is therefore important that we understand the role they play. In general they may be classified as positive—joy, love, confidence, for example—or negative—sadness, fear, anxiety, hatred. For the most part it is the negative emotions which have excessive effects. Fear can nearly paralyze the will; hatred can issue in violence.

Emotions may be conscious or unconscious. Over the latter the control of the will is very limited, and the result may be distortions in our thinking. An excessive degree of unconscious emotion is, however, an abnormal state which will not exist in most of us. Emotions can, of course, be abnormal by way of deficiency also. We may fail to react in circumstances which call for a reaction: fear when there is real danger; anger when there is grave wrong to be righted; joy when there is occasion for gladness. We can bring ourselves closer to the norm, in most cases, by a growth in self-understanding. Conflicting urges may diminish our freedom, but they will not destroy it. In the end, man himself decides freely and follows his choice.

In all our endeavors to construct from within the liberty which is ours as children of God we shall have the help of divine grace. The virtues of faith, hope, and love infused into the soul enable the mind and will to operate habitually on the supernatural level, in such a way, indeed, that God is in the background of our decisions. Thus is our freedom indirectly guided. In addition we receive the transitory help of actual graces, through the sacraments, or as assistance is needed in the events of life. Sometimes one is conscious of the aid of grace, at other times not. God always respects the human faculties which he has given us and works through them.

We shall encounter obstacles to the acceptance of normal responsibility. They are in the main four: fear, inertia, exhaustion, and excessive pressure from persons in authority. Becoming aware of these impediments will help us to guard against them.

Those of us who are charged with the training of the young, either as parents or teachers, can do much towards the formation of responsible freedom in the rising generation. In the home parents can teach by example in their own conscientious carrying out of their duties and also by the affectionate discipline whereby they train their children to accept responsibility for work suitable for their respective degrees of maturity. It is important that the children should have all possible freedom in carrying out their undertakings, that they should have the opportunity to experiment and to learn, if need be, from their mistakes. Standards of achievement should always be related to the capacities of the individual: the point is that the work should contribute to personal development. In families, as in other communities, there is always the danger that some will assume an excessive work load while others, through lack of confidence, laziness, or resentment at not getting a particular job, may fail to cooperate as fully as they should. Of course, persons differ in the matter of energy, too, and this should be taken into account.

Schools should continue the same kind of responsibility formation by setting definite standards in studies, by allowing student participation in the care of the classroom, the school building and grounds, and by extracurricular activities which develop initiative.

It should be made clear to the growing generation that life is not always easy, that doing our duty may sometimes entail sacrifice, that respecting the rights of others may sometimes be costly to ourselves.

Our essential role as Christians in the modern world as in the past is to cooperate with Christ our Brother in carrying forward and completing the redemption of the world. In him we are committed to teach, to guide, and to sanctify our fellow men.

Teaching is a service of love which involves no pretension of superiority with regard to our neighbor. It involves in the first place a witnessing to the gifts we have received from God, a reality which is communicated by our good example, our sincerity and warmth and candor in the exchange of ideas. There will also be circumstances in which we are able to guide others, with respect and love, by our counsel. It is possible for us to make our influence felt in whatever sector of life we find ourselves, with the result that the Christian leaven will be working in the areas of education, business, government, for the restoration of society to Christ.

Finally, our duty to sanctify others is not less real, and it does not depend on the achievement of perfection in ourselves. Through what we are, if we are living as closely as we are able to God, through little things we do, we can help others to dispose themselves to receive God's grace. Community worship and group prayer obtain many graces from God for all the members of the group. Indeed, only God can measure the effect of all we do for others, for it is to such an extent his doing, not ours. We read in *Mystici Corporis*: "No prayer is said, no good is done, without its effects on the entire Mystical Body."

But our responsibility does not end with the relationships which belong to our family, neighborhood, and professional life. We are under an obligation to inform ourselves with regard to those areas in society in which freedom is threatened by poverty, discrimination, or injustice of any kind. Today we are feeling the impact of such an avalanche of information about social problems of every class and nation all over the world that the danger is we shall yield to apathy, feeling that the task of coping with all this must be left to governments and other large institutions. But not being able to do everything does not excuse us from doing the something which is within our capacities in local circumstances. On the municipal, state, and national levels we can make thoughtful use of our political power as voters. We can discover and cooperate with those organizations which are concerned with reversing some of the injustices of society or caring for the most needy.

It is the great irony or our time, when we have achieved a greater mastery of the earth's resources than earlier in history and are in the process of exploring other planets, that the burden of suffering humanity seems more overwhelming than ever before. And the complexity of the world's organization has become such that whatever action we undertake to alleviate the suffering is done with the risk of failure. This is something the Christian must see in the light of the Beatitudes; for Our Lord did not say, Blessed are the successful, but Blessed are the merciful, for they shall obtain mercy.

CHAPTER 6

Initiative and Collegiality

The French philosopher P. J. Proudhon, who greatly influenced the thinking of Karl Marx, dreamed in his earliest writings of a society governed exclusively by laws, a society which, because of being perfectly governed by laws, would not need any authority (*Idée générale de la Révolution au XIXe siècle*, 1851). Later he changed his mind. In *Du Principe fédératif* (1863) he recognized the permanent necessity of authority as a principle of arbitration for certain cases not provided for by law. In the same way, in our time, the Protestant community of Taizé began with the idea of having neither rule nor authority, but within a few years accepted the practical necessity of both.

In modern times there exists among some people the vague belief that social progress depends fundamentally upon the increase of freedom, with a corresponding decrease of authority. So it would be good to ask, "What is authority? What is its function in community? How do initiative and freedom harmonize with authority?"

Authority is an active and directive power in a group which resides in a person or persons and is exercised through a command which another person by a practical judgement freely accepts as a norm for acting. Both persuasion and coercion are instruments of authority, but they are not authority. In part, authority only replaces the lack of internal evidence about a truth or replaces the lack of adequate knowledge or self-control in a person who has to act. In this sense it is limited and, up to a certain point, the extent of authority necessary in a given community or group is inversely proportioned to the development reached in the group and in the persons and subgroups which compose it.

Essentially, the function of authority is to assure unity of action in a united group. In a community of any kind it must also help the members achieve mutual affection, trust, and service. Since the unity of action necessary for the common good is always in danger, if all the members of the community are not in agreement, authority is an essential need and in no way accidental. So the necessity of authority is nothing less than a metaphysical consequence of the nature of things, a thing absolutely good in itself and rooted in the very being, in the metaphysical goodness, of nature. Being essentially the indispensable prudence of the community in its communitarian action, authority is a good and permanent source of social unity seeking the common good.

Therefore, we have to be cautious of the excessively rationalistic or legalistic mentality that does not want to accept the inescapable mystery of the contingent, the uncertain, the unpredictable, which has a very large part both in the physical world and in the human. Actually, the norms of community life have to spring from human nature and in this sense are prior to the consideration of any personal criterion. So these basic norms have to be discovered and recognized rather than given and promulgated, since they express nothing less than the universal and necessary aspects of the social beings we are.

In order that the basic norms of community or group life can be applied effectively and peacefully, the members have to grow as human persons to the point where their self-mastery permits them to seek the common good first of all, and not only their personal good. With this degree of freedom controlling selfish desires, the norms necessary for group life are already incorporated into the personality of the members and all can cooperate freely and intelligently with others in attaining common interests, without harming their authentic personal autonomy.

In this sense, with an increase in inner freedom, there is also progress in the life of the community and coercion is replaced more and more by persuasion, and there is less and less need for the exercise of authority. The essential function of authority, however, remains, since it has to unite the community in its living and acting in spite of the inevitable differences among members. But the more effectively united in its common action a community becomes, the more perfect, happy, and free will the community be and the more the members will experience the presence of God among them.

On this basis we can make a summary involving three principles: First, the principle of authority: While the welfare of the community requires a common action, the unity of this common action has to be assured by the highest organs of the group. Secondly, the principle of autonomy and subsidiarity: While a task can be carried through by the initiative of the individual or of small group units, the performance of the task should be left to the initiative of the individual or small group unit. In this way the autonomy of the individual or of the lower social unity supplies and counterbalances the authority of the higher social unit. Thirdly, the principle of collegiality: Collegiality is a way of being and living in which the authority and co-responsibility reside in the community and function by means of the community. Taking into account these three principles, we may conclude that the problems of freedom and authority must finally be solved in a community of love.

However, other important factors enter into the matter of freedom and initiative. To understand them better we must begin with the collegiality of the Church.

> The order of bishops is the successor to the college of the apostles in teaching authority and pastoral rule; or, rather, in the episcopal order the apostolic body continues without a break. Together with its head, the Roman Pontiff, and never without this head, the episcopal order is the subject of supreme and full power over the universal Church. But this power can be exercised only with the consent of the Roman Pontiff. (Dogmatic Constitution on the Church, no. 22).

They possess this power because their office is in its origin sacramental rather than juridical:

> This sacred Synod teaches that by divine institution bishops have succeeded to the place of the apostles as shepherds of the Church . . . . But episcopal consecration, together with the office of sanctifying, also confers the offices of teaching and governing. (These, however, of their very nature, can be exercised only in hierarchical communion with the head and the members of the college.) (Ibid nos. 20, 21)

Hence papal power does not reduce the bishops to being mere officials of the pope. And the power of the bishops does not derogate papal primacy. Rather we have here a unique structure of authority that is not strictly either monarchical or démocratic but collegial. Collegiality belongs to the Church as such and not simply to one part of it, i.e. to the episcopal body. It would be well to repeat that the power of a bishop is not a part of papal power, nor is it a mere delegation of the pope, but is possessed independently of the pope because of its sacramental origin, even though it cannot be exercised independently of him.

The members of the Church, as members, form a college which is at once similar to the episcopal college and distinct from it. The office of the laity is also sacramental rather than juridical in its origin. Whether he receives baptism and confirmation from the pope, from a bishop, or from a priest matters little. His stature as a Christian is not by this fact essentially heightened, for it is through Christ that he has been made new. Just as a bishop is not in his office by any human power, so neither is a layman charged with an office in the Church simply at the pleasure, however reasonable, of his ecclesiastical superiors. Rather it is Christ who has given him what he has and what he is. The ecclesiastical superiors have been no more than the instruments of Our Lord.

What is the authority of the layman in the Church? In the first place, the layman is not a passive person in the Church.

> Scripture declares that all brethren in Christ are called to the inheritance of sonship, all form God's holy house, his own holy people (1 Pt 2:5, 9f: 1 Cor 3:16f; Eph 2:19-22; Heb 10:21f). The word layman therefore means positively that the baptized person (thus sanctified in principle and favored with the very life of God) who is a member,

not a mere object of the Church, has an active function and responsibility, belongs to the holy people of God (1 Pt 2:10), must bear
witness by his life (and thus also by what he says) to God's grace
in Christ as the triumphant redemption of the world and all men;
he shares in the Church's task of taking up, elevating and fulfilling
man's purely human vocation in all spheres of human life (culture
and history) in the expectation and acceptance of the kingdom
of God. It is his responsibility to join in the celebration of the
sacrifice of the Church (Eucharist) as a member of the whole cele-
brant body, to undertake the share that concrete circumstances
indicate is his in the Church's total task and its external missionary
endeavor. The layman is also, by the *direct* favor and mission of
God, the potential vehicle of charisms by which God blesses and
guides his Church, however willingly and obediently the layman
adapts his charism to the general life of the Church, submitting
it to the "discerning of spirits" by the universal Church's higher
and more comprehensive charism in both its hierarchical and free
forms.[1]

Responsibility, however, does not guarantee official authority,
even though it implies some kind of authority. The layman could
not be merely an executor of detailed commands. The reason
is that "the lay apostolate is a participation in the saving mission
of the Church itself. Through their baptism and confirmation,
all are commissioned to that apostolate by the Lord Himself"
(Constitution on the Church, no. 33). Moreover, Vatican Council
II informs us that the Holy Spirit,

alloting His gifts "to each as he will" (1 Cor 12:11), distributes
special graces among the faithful of every rank. By these gifts He
makes them fit and ready to undertake the various tasks of offices
advantageous for the renewal and upbuilding of the Church,
according to the words of the Apostle: "To each person the manifestation of the Spirit is given for the common good" (1 Cor 12:7).
These charismatic gifts, whether they be the most outstanding or
the more simple and widely diffused, are to be received with thanksgiving and consolation, for they are exceedingly suitable and useful
for the needs of the Church. (Ibid., no. 12)

In this same document we also read:

The holy People of God shares also in Christ's prophetic office.
It spreads abroad a living witness to Him, especially by means

of a life of faith and charity and by offering to God a sacrifice of praise, the tribute of lips which give honor to his name (cf. Heb 13:15). The body of the faithful as a whole, anointed as they are by the Holy One (cf. 1 Jn 2:20), *cannot err in matters of belief.* Thanks to a supernatural sense of the faith which characterizes the people as a whole, it manifests this unerring quality when, "from the bishops down to the last member of the laity" (St. Augustine, *"De praed. sanct."* 14,27:PL 44,980), it shows universal agreement in matters of faith and morals. (Ibid., no. 12)

The outstanding thing in these citations is that, while the discernment of the authenticity of the charismatic or prophetic powers pertains to the hierarchy, the powers themselves pertain to the laity by their own right. So their role in the Church is not merely to be active, not merely to carry out their responsibilities. It is all this and more. It is the exercise of powers which they possess independently of any delegation by the clergy. The laity are laity sacramentally through the direct favor and mission of God by means of their baptism and confirmation.

For these reasons, since authority is given to the entire Church and to each member in it, according to the distribution of the Holy Spirit, no Christian as Christian could be subject to any absolute and unlimited authority, invested in a human being, because he shares through Christ the very authority of God. So there is reason for saying that according to the New Testament all the orders of authority in the Church, minor or major, are received immediately from Christ. Moreover, they are received and exercised in the context of the Church just as it is in itself as a totality and in all its members and as invested with the messianic authority of Christ. Thus it is that the entire people of God, all the faithful (and not only the hierarchy), is infallible in matters of faith when they agree with each other and with the hierarchy.

So it is clear that collegiality is not limited to the bishops but is rather the very structure of the Church itself, even though the collegiality of the people of God as a whole is not the same kind as that of the bishops. The important thing is that the opinions of the bishops do not have force simply because the pope agrees with them, even though, paradoxically, they would not have force if the pope did not agree with them. In a similar way, the opinions of the entire body of the faithful (in matters of faith) do not have force simply because the hierarchy agrees with them, even though they would not have force if the hierarchy declared them erroneous. Power is given to the entire Church, i.e. to the people of God united among themselves. In other words, collegiality depends intimately upon the communion of all men within the Church.

At this point it would be good to ask, To what extent is it actually recognized that Christians have authority by their own right? Among those in authority who are alert to current trends there is agreement about some or all of the following points: application of the principle of subsidiarity, conscientious consulting at all levels, encouragement of all to express even strongly at times, their ideas, fostering initiative, openness and frankness in dealing with everyone, courtesy and understanding in giving directives, treating everybody as adults, thinking of authority as service rather than as power. All of these attitudes and practices, however, could exist in an absolute monarchy, for they say nothing about authority shared with the community as its own right. The bibical and conciliar attitude demands even more.

The Church is neither monarchy, nor oligarchy nor democracy, but a community essentially distinct and apart from any of these. It is the people of God which in its totality shares the messianic and prophetic authority of Christ. As members of the people of God, those in authority and those subject to it are essentially equal, as are the Father and the Son. In the same way, spiritual fatherhood or motherhood is neither human nor divine but something essentially distinct. Not only the head but also each member in the community, by his own right, shares the authority of the community.

But how? How can decisions be shared in a Christian community without transforming the religious group into a democracy? It is not enough that the head recognize that by themselves the member or members probably could not see all the aspects of a matter. Neither is it enough that the opinions of the members be considered only because of their value. In order that the members can really share in the decisions of the community two things are necessary: first, the content of the opinions of the members has to have some part in the decisions of the heads; secondly, they have to have part, not only for their intrinsic value but also because they are the opinions of the members of the group.

Naturally, these two conditions do not exclude either the intrinsic value of the members' opinions or the desire to maintain harmony in the community. Neither is there excluded the possibility that, at times, the head and his board have to decide a matter on the basis of confidential information which cannot be shared for various motives of prudence, justice, or charity. What matters is this: the essence of shared authority is that an opinion has weight for the sole reason that it is the opinion of a member.

So we can be clear about certain differences that exist between authority exercised in the community of the Church and the same in a matrimonial or Christian community. In the Church it is mainly a descending movement from Christ and by means of the hierarchy to all the members of Christ with whom they are intimately and vitally linked, as the Constitution on the Church explains (no.21). But in a very real way, it is also a shared and horizontal authority, because the Holy Spirit speaks and acts through the members in order to achieve the common good. It is a sacramental community, that is, it is established and functions through the sacraments. On the other hand, a Christian community is not principally hierarchical, but essentially a brotherhood, a fraternity which is established and functions through voluntary agreement and personal initiative. Within the people of God and working through fraternal communication, the Christian community accomplishes its purposes by responding to the impulses of the Holy Spriit in the heart of the baptized. So the members of the brotherhood, by mutual assistance, seek the fullness of their existence in Christ. In the Church the help and the fullness come more directly from Christ. It is a matter of degree.

Hence authority in community does not depend on a sacramental grace. At the sacramental level there is nothing to distinguish head and members. Authority springs from the fundamental equality of all the baptized, who are brothers in Christ. As a consequence, the validity of the power of the head depends upon the free election of the members, upon the approval of a higher authority (which does not always have sacramental hierarchical authority, i.e., vicar general) and upon the head's fidelity to given constitutions that specify the limits of authority.

It is in place here to consider the purpose of those who enter a community. Mainly, their purpose is twofold: to live more united to God and to serve others in carrying out the work of the community. The head serves as a director for realizing these two ends. It is, however, the community of love and peace that is more important than anything. Therefore, there is great disillusionment and rebellion when the head is not adequate to the job or when there is neither affection nor reasonable order. The community is not formed around the head; rather the head is formed by the community and is at the center of all the impulses that come horizontally from the Lord by way of the members. So authority serves to direct the community itself and each member towards a deeper communion with God, towards a more intimate mutual communion among the members that harmonizes with the distinctive characteristics of each one, and towards the service of others.

We might add, parenthetically, that the democratic environment has been at its best a sign of the collegiality that needs to be functioning in our times. It is a "sign of the times."

It is important that authority be chosen in the most democratic way possible, with an absolute minimum of delegates-by-reason-of-office. Certainly, all authority is from God, but by way of all the members, by way of the brotherhood. The will of the members, legitimately expressed, confers the power to direct the community. Ecclesiastical approval confirms the election for the Christian community. It confirms also the rule that guides both the authority and the members in their communion with God, with one another, and with the people they serve.

Humanly speaking, each community of brothers or sisters requires a visible sign that at once expresses and promotes the communion among them. Authority offers this brotherly service by being the sign of Christ who gathers his brothers around himself in order to develop the natural and supernatural gifts that the Father committed to them. However, besides being the bond of brotherhood, the center of the search for union with God and the promoter of fidelity to the Holy Spirit, the head has to radiate peace and joy. Therefore, he cannot be distanced from the community, much less behave with pride, contempt, or bad temper. Rather, he has to be very humanly one with the brothers, sharing as a brother all their sorrows and joys. In other words, co-responsibility implies also the capacity to get along well with people and to be pleasantly agreeable.

It is not enough, however, to say that authority is service. There is still more: Authority is not a closed and impenetrable circle. It is a service that seeks the union of all with the Eternal Father. Jesus prayed: "I pray also for those who will believe in me through their word, that all may be one as you, Father, are in me, and I in you" (Jn 7:20-21). Jesus is the Head of the new people of God precisely because he is the servant of the Father. It will be that way until the end of time, as St. Paul says: "When, finally, all has been subjected to the Son, he will then subject himself to the One who made all things subject to him, so that God may be all in all" (1 Cor 15:28).

So we find a fraternal service that is open and transparent not only to the light that comes through communion with the brothers but also to the full responsibility that results from communion with the Eternal Father. The role of authority as service is to help others discern and follow the still higher authority which it serves. Therefore, changes and assignments should be made in full communion both with the distinct personality of each member and with the will of the Eternal Father. For this theological reason, it is advisable, as far as possible, to consult with each member before making changes and assignments. This does not exclude the physical, mental, or emotional sickness which can twist the judgment of the person concerned and thus hinder the light of grace, nor the exceptional cases in which the true common welfare has rights that are prior to those of the individual. The real common good is also the good of the individual.

Theologically, therefore, authority can be exercised only by means of dialogue. It presupposes a continual intercommunication and, consequently, it demands an absolute respect for the fundamental human worth and for the sacramental power of each member of the group. Essentially, it is an authority of dialogue and communion. It is precisely in the light of these facts and of the present emphasis on the collegiality and subsidiarity of Vatican II, and not on monarchical ideas and practices of the past, that one must interpret paragraph 14 of the Vatican document "Appropriate Renewal of Religious Life." Only in this way are the following words applicable: "Lived in this manner, religious obedience will not diminish the dignity of the human person but will rather lead it to maturity in consequence of that enlarged freedom which belongs to the sons of God."

It follows that co-responsibility, far from threatening authority, rather expresses the nature of the brotherhood that is the heart of the Gospel. Being the servant of that design which the Father has written in the heart of each of his children, the head of the community has even more dignity. It is only that the leader has to be more concerned with listening, very humbly, fraternally and attentively, to the suggestions of the creative Spirit made in the hearts of the members. It is up to the leader to consult, dialogue, weigh and distinguish. Finally, it is part of the service of the group leader of the brotherhood to accept, reject, or modify in the most agreeable way possible the suggestions of all, to make sure they harmonize with the designs of God.

The members, for their part, exercise their initiative and freedom by participating actively and agreeably in the dialogue, for in this way they contribute to the good of the brotherhood. No one can hinder the members in their open dialogue, since a community is above all a mutual compenetration of understanding and affection. Moreover, theologically, collegiality and subsidiarity forbid heaping upon the head so many detailed responsibilities that they hinder his authentic function of securing the fidelity of the community to the call of the Lord. In this way, also, there is avoided an excess of detailed laws in any constitutions or guiding principles the group might adopt.

Finally, where it might seem necessary, instead of asking permission for many little things, members could give a responsible report periodically about what has happened, since, even though many times it is more difficult to act by one's own initiative, this will be a way of developing more fully the freedom of the spirit that marks a Christian adult.

Following this same theological line, we see that all legislative power should not be left to the heads of a community. The supreme ordinary legislative power is always the general chapter. And in our democratic age there should be a permanent committee, chosen by the general chapter, with legislative powers (sometimes called the implementation committee) which would apply through administrative decrees the will of the community expressed in the general chapter. Any member can propose legislative matters to the permanent committee. To avoid conflicts, a member of the governing board could head this committee. By this procedure collegiality and subsidiarity would function better, and there would be the flexibility that is so indispensable in apostolic works. At least everything possible should be decided by the vote of the majority.

In order to encourage all to use well the different gifts given by God to all the community through each member and to maintain unity of life and action, there has to be also an executive power. This is the role of the leaders. Hence, their prime virtue has to be their prudent obedience in carrying out the will of the community expressed through the general chapter and the constitutions. The executive power can be distributed among several special committees.

When a decision is made by the vote of the majority, the head of the group has to put it into effect, and he has the full power necessary to put the decision into effect. Normally, the system of deciding many things by vote of the majority demands a careful selection of members and also a very high human and spiritual level in them as well as in the general life of the group. In a community there will be an excellent spirit and great effectiveness in accomplishing the goals of the group only if the qualities of the members are exceptional. Otherwise, the community descends to mediocrity or worse.

In this democratic age some groups are sharing authority still more by means of a judicial committee or board of reconciliation or arbitration. This board functions as the judicial branch of the government of the group. Thoroughly spelled out by the chapter are the specific purposes, the principles, functions, types of cases, authority of the board, methods of election, procedures, archives, appeals, etc. Well selected and functioning well, such a board of arbitration could relieve the executive branch of much work, assure justice to the members, and inspire more respect for community life.

In any case, while the special charisma given to a particular community can serve throughout many periods of social growth, its interpretation and application has to harmonize with the needs of the moment. So it is not sufficient to discover the initial spiritual inspiration of the community. That original impulse must function with the graces that the Holy Spirit is offering at present. "No man pours new wine into old wineskins. No, new wine is poured into new skins" (Mk 2:22). One cannot put the new graces in the old structures. We have to seek new structures for the new graces. In this way we participate in the Incarnation, which continues through new members and new ways of carrying out the mission of Christ. We need a strong faith in the Providence of God working through human goodness.

Only God, by his very being and nature, is completely free of all structure, since he alone is absolutely and perfectly open at all times to all that exists in every creature. In God there is no time: neither past, present, nor future. Human persons are finite and limited; they can only respond in a particular way to the particular circumstances that affect them. So the development of human personalities requires a development and adjustment of the structures that surround them. To try to be totally free of all structures is the ancient temptation of everybody, the temptation to play at being God. While some structures serve a purpose, we must, at the same time, transcend the structures themselves and never be their slaves. Our bodily existence forces us to seek the infinite by means of the finite and limited. Silence and various ways of praying open us to God.

In community life, structures serve a purpose only when there is a good relationship between the members. There could still be a lot of resentment in a community with very little structure. Between free human persons there should be only such a minimum of structures as will help the community to be a home, a family that is pleasantly agreeable, affectionate, an experience capable of satisfying the spiritual, social, educational, affective, and physical needs of the members. In this way, initiative, freedom, and authentic collegiality harmonize and grow together.

> A sense of the dignity of the human person has been impressing itself more and more deeply on the consciousness of contemporary man. And the demand is increasingly made that men should act on their own judgment, enjoying the making use of responsible freedom, not driven by coercion but motivated by a sense of duty. The demand is also made that constitutional limits be set to the powers of government, in order that there be no encroachment on the rightful freedom of the person and of association. (Vatican II, Decree on Religious Liberty, no. 1)

[1] K. Rahner and H. Vorgrimler, *Theological Dictionary* (New York: Herder and Herder, 1965), p. 259.

II

Biblical

CHAPTER 7

Jesus Is Lord

We find Jesus as Lord in the opening words of that beautiful theological poem, the Prologue of St. John's Gospel:

> In the beginning was the Word; and the Word was in God's presence, and the Word was God. He was present to God in the beginning. Through him all things came into being, and apart from him nothing came to be. Whatever came to be in him, found life, life for the light of men. The light shines on in darkness, a darkness that did not overcome it. (Jn 1:1-5)

The Father eternally utters his Word, and the Word is God. The Word is the light of men, the light which is life.

Again, in St. Paul's Epistle to the Colossians, we read:

> He is the image of the invisible God, the first-born of all creation; for in him all things were created, in heaven and on earth, visible and invisible . . . all things were created through him and for him. He is before all things, and in him all things hold together. (1:15-17, RSV)

The reality of Christ's Lordship is this: If we were able in a single vision to see the whole universe—past, present, and future—we should see everything depending for its being on Christ and taking its meaning from him. This is the reality on which all our relationships—with God, with the world, with ourselves and each other—must be founded. Our continued growth depends on the deepening of our understanding of such

69

complex and interwoven relationships and the sensitizing of our response to them; for there is a certain deadliness about taking things for granted: if our approach to reality is static, there is no dynamic response, no searching intercommunication either with other persons or with our surroundings. We can never stand still. If we are not moving forward, growing, expanding our powers and deepening our understanding by listening to ourselves as persons and sensitively responding in our relationship with God, with other people, and with the world that is always touching and affecting us, then regression and atrophy take over and we begin to die. And the source of our growth is Christ. So Teilhard de Chardin writes: "May the risen Christ keep us young, that is, optimistic, active, smiling, perceptive."

The first question we should ask ourselves, therefore, when we review our lives is, What do I think of Christ? Taking myself as I am, who is Jesus to me personally at this moment in my life? How am I responding to him? What is the depth and quality of my faith, of my hope, of my love? Do I think of Jesus, perhaps, as a great man—even the most perfect man? Jesus wished to draw us, through his perfect humanity, to the experience of himself as God. Do I think principally of Jesus' message, of his teaching? Do I respond more to his miracles, the marvelous things he was always doing, with the hope that perhaps he might work a miracle in my own life?

With regard to Jesus' earthly life, we must, if we compare it to the extraordinarily penitential life of John the Baptist, think of it as on the surface less remarkable. Jesus grew up as an ordinary person, the son of the village carpenter, an apprentice and then a master carpenter, who supported his mother; a man who in his public life had friends who welcomed him to their table. Indeed he was so often at banquets that his enemies accused him of being a glutton and a wine-drinker. True, there were the forty days of fasting and prayer in the desert in preparation for his public ministry; then, in his public life, he suffered misunderstandings, contradictions and insults, disappointments and rejection; and at last the cataclysmic closing of his life with his passion and crucifixion. The life, ending in tragedy, of a great teacher who loved his fellow men—am I aware, in my relationship with him, that the man who led this life and died this death is God?

For St. John, who spent his long life in the contemplation of Christ's divinity, salvation is enlightenment: it is the work of the Word who is the Light. This Light is the life of men. That the Word was made flesh is the central mystery of our salvation. Adhering to Christ in faith, we pass from darkness into light, from death to life.

We need light for life even in the natural order. Even the creatures living in the darkest depths of the ocean sustain their life on those other living things which receive their life through light from above. Everything we are in the uttermost depths of our being depends on the light, the participation in the divine life, which comes to us from Christ who is God.

In and through Christ we know God as Father, and through him we go to the Father. Through Christ we receive our life; and in that sense it is possible to say that there is an aspect of fatherhood in Christ, our redeemer.

In his discourse at the Last Supper, Jesus said to the apostles: "I have called you friends, for all that I have heard from my Father I have made known to you." Do I love Jesus as a friend?

It may be, as we review our attitude towards Jesus, that we shall discover in ourselves the need for a true biblical repentance, a rethinking of the whole direction of our lives in relation to him. For it is possible for our response to him to be negative—the response that is called sin. It is interesting to note that just when the modern world seemed to have established the idea that there was no such thing as sin and that the very notion of it was harmful to human personality, there has come a strong biblical revival, and with it a relearning of the meaning of sin from God's own word. And those who privately or in groups are once more reading the Bible are discovering, along with the consolation they receive, that "God's word is living and effective, sharper than any two-edged sword. It penetrates and divides soul and spirit, joints and marrow; it judges the reflections and thoughts of the heart" (Heb 4:12).

The biblical concept of sin, as the negative response of man to God, presupposes the positive aspects of all that God has done for man through salvation history. The books of Moses always remain God's personal word, addressed to a people he loved with an entirely gratuitous, unearned, and unaccountable love. Sin in the biblical concept is, in part, a turning aside from this love-given word; it is simply missing the goal, deviating from the right way of friendship with God, renouncing happiness by failing to keep his covenant of love.

The biblical concept of sin is also the rebellion of the first man, because all of us are God's chosen people. There is only one people of God, the people that began with the opening stages of sacred history and reaches until the end of time. The eldest son has very special and solemn obligations as well as special privileges. Sin is a rebellion of the first-born against the Father.

In the biblical sense, sin is also infidelity—the infidelity of the bride to the monogamous spouse. God is a jealous God because he loves. Such a concept of God as jealous is caught up in the twofold mystery of who God is and of how to express who he is. Strictly speaking, God does not need man. So why should he be jealous? However, taking ourselves where we are in our very concrete way of thinking of things and our need to reduce them to bite size, a manageable size, we know that God is greatly concerned about us; he does not want us to be giving our love, our loyalty, our service, to anyone but himself.

In the Old Testament sin is also a breach of the covenant, an infidelity to love; that is, to the covenant which was a gift of God's goodness and obliged by love rather than by justice, even though it was a bilateral contract (Hos 8:1). Without having to, God committed himself to man's protection and care. Sin is infidelity to love, which is the giving of one's whole self. Therefore, in a sense, sin gets into the blood-line and make the sinner, in its biblical meaning, a son of wrath. This is why Jesus said to the Pharisees, "The father you spring from is the devil" (Jn 8:44).

Sin is also a lie, a deception. The sinner acts deceitfully. He pretends to be something he is not. While a lie is a denial of reality by speech, sin is a denial of reality by action.

Iniquity means that reality has become what it ought not to be. In the concrete, iniquity means "guilt," a distortion that remains as the result of an iniquitous action. And the damage of sin to the sinner is not only his liability before God but also the corruption of his own inner person (Ez 24:6).

Sin is often called folly, and the sinner a fool (Dt 32:6; Jer 4:22 and 5:21). Self-made fools are not treated with sympathy. Anyone who deliberately unleashes trouble is a fool, for sin is also trouble, affliction, sorrow. The sinner is a troublemaker, not only for himself but also for others.

The origin of sin is a lack of knowledge of God, but in the sense of refusing to know—i.e., a refusal to accept—God, to recognize God for all that he is (Hos 2:8 and 4:1,6). Historically, sin began with man's free choice when he was in his original condition of innocence without the burden of sin and evil desires. Though tempted by agents outside himself, he had the power to resist the temptation, but he yielded because he wanted something which was not his.

The result of sin is a curse. The first and dominant effect of sin is death. The sinner dies a little each time he sins. Moreover, once sin came into the world, it spread. In the eyes of God the earth was corrupt and full of lawlessness (Gn 6:11). Hence, guilt for sin was individual because men were free and personally responsible. "The Old Testament explanation of the mystery of evil is that there is no disaster or affliction in the personal or social life of man or in nature which is not to be attributed to the sin of man; no matter to what degree man suffers, it is no more than the just result of his deeds."[1]

Guilt for sin was also collective:

> The solidarity of the Israelites was based upon their physical descent from Abraham and further strengthened on Mount Sinai by their covenant relationship with Yahweh and their so-called spiritual marriage with him. Just as Adam, the head of the human race, left traces of his original sin upon all mankind, so, too, individual Israelites, because of their official position, committed particular transgressions that affected the collective guilt of the entire community. Thus, the violation of the ceremonial law by the high

priest incurred a sort of collective guilt on all people, whom he represented before God (Lv 4:3); the Israelites were punished for the sins of Achan (Jos 7:10-15); King David (2 Sm 24:10-17), King Achab (3 Kgs 17:1), King Manasses (4 Kgs 21:10-15, 23:26). Families were at times severely punished for the sins of their heads (Jeroboam I, 3 Kgs 14:10). Because of the massacres of the Gabaonites by King Saul, blood-guilt hung heavily upon his house and was finally expiated by a three-year famine in the days of King David (2 Sm 21:1). The Israelites were often admonished to repent and to acknowledge the collective guilt of their sins as well as those of their forefathers.[2]

In the Old Testament, even though God could intervene and prevent the consequences of sin; even though expiatory sacrifices were accepted as an intervention; and even though prayers and sorrow won reinstatement with God, still forgiveness did not automatically include the remission of punishment. This is evident from David's sin with Bathsheba (the baby died). Punishment of sin was not so much retribution "visited" upon the sinner as it was the normal consequence of sin running its course. The idea of temporal punishment due to sin echoes biblical doctrine.

In the New Testament sin is infidelity to Christ our Lord, to the incomparable love he shows us by laying down his life for us and being in himself our new covenant. So totally did he take our sins upon himself, so completely did he identify with us, in order to make reparation for us, that St. Paul is able to say, mysteriously: "For our sakes God made him who did not know sin, to be sin, so that in him we might become the very holiness of God" (2 Cor 5:21).

In the New Testament the focus is on Jesus as the conqueror of sin. This in no way diminishes the malice of sin as it is conceived in the Old Testament; rather it emphasizes the divine nature of Jesus' saving action. In the Old Testament God could deliver man from sin: in the New Testament God does deliver man from sin.

In Matthew, Mark and Luke, Jesus is the friend of sinners who calls them to repentance (Mt 9:10, and 11:19; Lk 7:34; 15:1-2; 19:7). His kindness makes real the divine mercy and readiness to forgive. Sins come from the heart and they alone can defile

men (Mt 15:19-20; Mk 7:20-22). Sin is the wandering of the son
from his father's house (Lk 15:18-21). The sinner need only ask
for forgiveness to receive it. And there is joy in heaven over
the repentance of a sinner (Lk 15:7,10).

John makes clearer the malice of sin. Sin is lawlessness (1
Jn 3:4) and unrighteousness (1 Jn 5:17). He who sins is from
the devil (1 Jn 3:8) and is the slave of sin (Jn 8:34). Sin is the
lust of the flesh and of the eyes; it is the pride of life (1 Jn
2:16). In John, sin more commonly means not the single act,
but a state or condition induced by the evil action. Like the
guilt of the Old Testament, the sin endures in the sinner. Sin
is often opposed to truth, just as in the Old Testament the sin
is a lie. The result of sin is death (1 Jn 5:16).

In St. Paul, the entire Gentile world is corrupted by sin because
they refused to recognize God (Rom 1:18-32). While sin is a
deliberate action, it is also a state, a condition, the human condition. Sin reigns as a power (Rom 5-8). When the first man sinned
he broke off harmonious relations with God for the entire race.
Sin brings death. All men die. Hence all men are sinners, even
though they may not have sinned personally. While he explicitly
rejects the idea that men share in some way in the personal
action of their ancestor, Paul points out that they do share in
the condition which results from that action, the condition of
being "enemies of God" (Rom 5:10). This can be understood
only in the light of the twofold biblical belief in the solidarity
of the race and the representative role of the individual: thus
the first man, Adam, stands for the race of men; thus St. Paul
calls Christ the Second Adam. The prophecy of the coming of
the Redeemer in the Old Testament is fulfilled in the New (cf.
Is 40-55, from which there are quotations in Mt 8:17; 12:18-21;
Lk 22:37; Rom 15:21; 4:25; also at the baptism of Jesus, Mt 3:17;
Mk 1:11; Lk 3:22). "Were it not for the solidarity of the representative, it would be impossible for the deliverance to be as total
as the curse."[3]

In the Epistle to the Hebrews we read:

> When in former times God spoke to our forefathers, he spoke
> in fragmentary and varied fashion through the prophets. But in
> the final age he has spoken to us in the Son whom he has made

heir to the whole universe, and through whom he created all orders of existence: the Son who is the effulgence of God's splendor and the stamp of God's very being, and sustains the universe by his word of power. When he had brought about the purgation of sins, he took his seat at the right hand of Majesty on high . . . . In subjecting all things to him, he left nothing that is not subject. But in fact we do not yet see all things in subjection to man. In Jesus, however, we do see one who for a short while was made lower than the angels, crowned now with glory and honor because he suffered death, so that, by God's gracious will, in tasting death he should stand for us all.[4]

Man's destined grandeur as sovereign of the universe is shown in Jesus, whose conquest of death has given him Lordship of the whole creation:

Man who had lost immortality by disobedience had to attain the predestined glory of his adoptive sonship by treading the painful way of obedience. Hence the "grace of God" was that the Man who recapitulates humanity "should taste death for all" (2:9). As the Author of human salvation, the Son, according to a plan of solidarity with our condition, was to attain his own glory, the perfection of his Saviorship and the sympathy of his priestly quality by undergoing sufferings and death. He could not, of course, give up his natural Sonship and become an adopted Son, but he could and did become the brother of those called by God into participation in his Sonship. In the Incarnation he finds fellowship of flesh and blood with men, makes his own their attitude of filial creature-confidence towards God, and submits to all the physical debt of human guilt, even to death. Thus the devil's empire of death was broken and the black slavery of mortality undone. Man was weak, and the Savior became weak; man was subject to pain, and the Savior submitted to pain; man was liable to mental anguish, and the Savior experienced anguish. By the Incarnation therefore he bound himself to us in a full program of *sympathy*. The knowledge that he sinlessly experienced all the painful trials of sinful flesh gives sinners every confidence in this faithful High Priest.[5]

Jesus is our joy. "All this I tell you that my joy may be yours and your joy may be complete" (Jn 15:11). Do we, in the misdt of the inevitable disorders and sufferings of this world, preserve the peace and joy which belong to a Christ-centered universe? He has said: "No follower of mine shall ever walk in darkness;

no, he shall possess the light of life" (Jn 8:12). Do we live as persons reborn into the risen life of Christ, as new creatures in Christ at a level and in a mode of life beyond the merely natural, beyond what can be seen and touched? How deeply does our faith look into the heart of things, renewed by the resurrection?

This Jesus who is our Lord is to be trusted; he heals and renews our lives with the constant enrichment of both our human and Christian person. He is himself the Way we walk towards the fulfillment of our human person in eternal happiness. "Everyone begotten of God conquers the world, and the power that has conquered the world is this faith of ours. Who, then, is the conqueror of the world? The one who believes that Jesus is the Son of God" (1 Jn 5:4-5).

[1] J. L. McKenzie, *Dictionary of the Bible* (Milwaukee: Bruce, 1965), p. 819.

[2] *Catholic Bible Encyclopedia;* ed. John E. Steinmuller and Kathryn Sullivan (New York: Wagner, 1956), Old Testament, p. 1013.

[3] McKenzie, *op. cit.*, p. 821.

[4] Heb 1:1-3;2:9 quoted from *The New English Bible* (New York: Oxford University Press and Cambridge University Press, 1961). Copyright The Delegates of the Oxford University Press and the Syndics of the Cambridge University Press, 1961.

[5] *A Catholic Commentary on Holy Scripture* (New York: Nelson, 1953), 930a, p. 1156.

CHAPTER 8

Jesus Is Our Covenant

In Isaiah 42:6 is introduced that mysterious Suffering Servant who is a foreshadowing in the Old Testament of the Messiah who would be the covenant[1] between God and men: "I the Lord have called you in justice, and taken you by the hand, and preserved you. And I have given you for a covenant of the people, for a light of the Gentiles." The New Testament, in the prologue to John's Gospel, describes the coming of the Messiah himself:

> He was in the world, and through him the world was made, yet the world did not know who he was. To his own he came, yet his own did not accept him. Anyone who did accept him he empowered to become children of God. These are they who believed in his name—who were begotten not by blood, nor by carnal desires nor by man's willing it but by God. The Word became flesh and made his dwelling among us, and we have seen his glory: the glory of an only Son coming from the Father, filled with enduring love. John testified to him by proclaiming: "This is he of whom I said, 'The one who comes after me ranks ahead of me, because he was before me.' " Of his fullness we have all had a share—love following upon love. But while the law was given through Moses, this enduring love came through Jesus Christ. No one has ever seen God. It is God, the only Son, ever at the Father's side, who has revealed him. (Jn 1:10-18)

It is the history of every generation that the goodness of a person or a movement which means the introduction of something new is recognized only with great reluctance and often too late to be of benefit to either. In religious matters, above all, the reluctance to accept new ideas and ways is very stubborn. To some extent this is understandable because everything religious is in some way associated with the unchangeable and eternal nature of God. Religious ideas and practices, moreover, have often been officially sanctioned in one way or another. They are also deeply involved with our feelings, and those feelings, in turn, have been reinforced by a specific pattern of theological reasoning. So it was in the time of Jesus. Though he came not to set aside the Law but to fulfill it, his teaching inevitably involved change which was seen as revolutionary.

Even for those who did accept him, a manifestation of the Holy Spirit was needed before they were able to go forth with courage to exercise the power which was theirs through Christ. On Ascension Day, Jesus told his apostles to wait in Jerusalem for the fulfillment of his Father's promise: "Within a few days you will be baptized with the Holy Spirit" (Acts 1:5). Then on Pentecost Sunday came that great outpouring of the Holy Spirit which transformed the apostles, setting them speaking in tongues about the marvels which God had accomplished through Jesus.

In our own time, Pope John XXIII prayed that there would be a new Pentecost, and we should not be surprised that his prayer has been answered. Today a powerful outpouring of the Holy Spirit is sweeping through our whole culture and through every religious denomination. We must cultivate an openness towards whatever the Holy Spirit is trying to say to us and be ready to be transformed by him, lest we be like the people of Our Lord's time, so entrenched in their fixed attitudes that they did not know who the Savior was.

They should have been prepared for his coming, for throughout sacred history God has shown himself in various ways. In a concrete, practical way he first made the covenant of nature with Noah in which he forbade, on man's side, the eating of meat with the blood in it (Gn 9:4) and the act of homicide. And as a pledge to his people that he would never again destroy the earth by a flood, he put a sign of his covenant in the sky:

"I will set my bow in the clouds, and it shall be the sign of a covenant between me, and between the earth. And when I shall cover the sky with clouds, my bow shall appear in the clouds; . . . and I shall see it, and shall remember the everlasting covenant" (Gn 9:13-16). So whenever we see the exquisite colors of the rainbow up there—whether it is double or single, or when viewed from above in a plane appears as two arches lying flat or even as a complete circle—we should see it always in its religious meaning as the sign of that covenant. It is God's pledge to us.

Then there was the covenant of faith with Abraham which required that he should believe and do what God would ask of him. In terms of that covenant God put Abraham's faith to the test when he commanded him to sacrifice his dearly beloved only son, Isaac (for Ishmael had been borne to him by a concubine), through whom God had promised to make him the father of a great nation (Gn 22). Abraham obeyed, taking Isaac to the place of sacrifice, but God intervened to spare the boy's life. And he kept his promise to make Abraham, through Isaac, the father of a great nation: "By your descendants shall all the nations of the earth be blessed, because you have obeyed my voice" (Gn 22:18). The sign of that covenant of faith with Abraham was circumcision (Gn 17:10).

With Moses, God in his loving-kindness made the covenant of law, sealed with blood and requiring, on the side of the people, their obedience and loyalty. Its sign was the sabbath worship. This covenant, a preparation for the final covenant sealed with the blood of Jesus, is carried forward to our time in the words Jesus himself used as he transformed the substance of bread and wine at the Last Supper into the living substance of his human nature. In Exodus (ch. 24) we read of how Moses sent out young men "to sacrifice young bulls as peace offerings" (v. 5) and bring him the blood. Part of that blood he poured over the altar (which represented God) and the rest he sprinkled over the people, saying, as he did so: "This is the blood of the covenant" (v. 8). So it was a blood pact, a blood-sealed agreement between God and man. The contracting parties became one blood, one family. There was also a covenant meal shared with the Lord by Moses, Aaron and his sons, and the seventy elders who represented the entire people (Gn 24:9-11).

It was to this covenant in the past that Jesus referred when he said, "This is my blood, the blood of the covenant" (Mt 26:28). "This cup is the new covenant in my blood, which will be shed for you" (Lk 22:20). So our new and eternal covenant is sealed not with the blood of animals but with the blood of Jesus himself. It is for this reason that there is so much stress upon the blood of Jesus in St. Paul (especially in Hebrews)[2], in St. John, and in the saints down the ages (Catherine of Siena, for example). His blood is not only one mode of the presence of Jesus, it is the culmination of a whole history of covenants between God and man and a sealing of the final covenant which Jesus voluntarily became from his first will-act to his death, resurrection, and ascension. This is the blood whose merits we claim when we pray to the Father in Jesus' name. "The blood of Jesus assures our entrance into the sanctuary" (Heb 10:19). This final covenant also had its signs, and those signs are the Eucharist, the Mass and the sacraments.

We stand, therefore, now in a personal covenanted relationship with God that is much more than a relationship of creature to a creator, student to teacher, or child to father. Our covenant is the Person of the God-man. Jesus is our covenant in his living Person. He is God's commitment to us and he is our commitment to God. Therefore, God's love is also a covenant love; it is a committed love. Given his commitment, then, God is as much obliged as we are to fulfill the conditions of the covenant. That is why we can pray with such absolute confidence. That is why Jesus wants us to invoke the covenant he is. "Whatsoever you ask the Father, he will give you in my name" (Jn 16:23). "If two of you join your voices on earth to pray for anything whatever, it shall be granted you by my Father in heaven" (Mt 18:19). This is what God prepared us for through Isaiah (42:6) and the Psalms. In Ps 25:14, "The friendship of the Lord is with those who fear him and his covenant for their instruction." In Ps 89:35, "I will not violate my covenant; the promise of my lips I will not alter."

So we stand before the Father, not with just ourselves speaking to God, nor merely with all the guarantees of God's love, mercy, and power and his desire to save man, however tremendous they already are. We have at every moment the action of the living covenant Jesus is. "Jesus, because he remains forever, has a priesthood which does not pass away. Therefore, he is always able to save those who approach God through him, since he forever lives to make intercession for them" (Heb 7:24-25). "This great confidence is ours through Christ. It is not that we are entitled of ourselves to take credit for anything. Our sole credit is from God, who has made us qualified ministers of a new covenant, a covenant not of a written law but of Spirit" (2 Cor 3:4-6; cf. Jer 31:33).

What is our covenant response? Are we faithful to Jesus our covenant? Do we really believe in him? Do we ask with the confidence that God has committed himself to be faithful to his covenant, that he has committed Jesus to be with us as our living mediator, that he has committed himself to Jesus to answer whatever we ask of him in Jesus' name? This confidence is important, because the one absolute power that God has given to us is the terrible power to say no to him. It is the terrible power to disbelieve God, the power to believe only in part or take what he says only half seriously.

The fact is that through this covenant we now are partners with God. He has put the wealth of divine goodness in our hands. Jesus has given us his power. "The man who has faith in me will do the works I do, and greater far than these" (Jn 14:12). He has given us his peace, the union and harmony of all things with God. "My peace is my gift to you" (Jn 14:27). He has given us his love. "As the Father has loved me, so I have loved you. Live on in my love" (Jn 15:9 and Rom 5:5). He has given us the Holy Spirit "whom the Father will send in my name" (Jn 14:26). He has given us his divine saving presence to unite us in love and to continue his work as mediator and witness. "I have given them the glory you gave me that they may be one as we are one—I living in them, you living in me—that their unity may be complete. So shall the world know that you sent me, and that you loved them as you loved me" (Jn 17:22-23).

Peace in the biblical sense is the working out of justice (Is 32:17), the setting of everything right within us and around us, the union and harmony of all things with God (Jn 14:27). Hence, the theology of liberation and the need to move beyond what we have always spoken of as a social justice at the philosophical level. We are now in a covenanted relationship with God and with one another. Jesus entered into this world to redeem not merely man but the whole universe. His work is a re-creation (Jn 1). In him everything was created and saved. "It pleased God to make absolute fullness reside in him and, by means of him, to reconcile everything in his person, both on earth and in heaven, making peace through the blood of his cross" (Col 1:19-20). All of us are looking forward to the culmination of Christ's work on the last day. In the meantime, we are committed as God's instruments to establish a justice which will bring true peace to men. This commitment implies the power to change social structures that hinder justice. That is our part and we are to take it very seriously because God has committed himself to do his part.

The condition God has placed is our faith. What kind of faith? The faith that knows with a deep, confident conviction that God intends to honor his commitment and that we can thank him at once for the answer already given. Failing in this kind of faith, we fail to keep our part of the covenant. To the blind men, Jesus said, " 'Are you confident I can do this?' 'Yes, Lord,' they told him. At that he touched their eyes and said, 'Because of your faith it shall be done to you'; and they recovered their sight" (Mt 9:28-30). To the hemorrhaging woman Jesus said, "Daughter, it is your faith that has cured you. Now go in peace" (Lk 8:48). "To the centurion Jesus said, 'Go home. It shall be done because you trusted.' That very moment the boy got better" (Mt 8:13). Jesus said, "Signs like these will accompany those who have professed their faith: they will use my name to expel demons, they will speak entirely new languages, they will be able to handle serpents, they will be able to drink deadly poison without harm, and the sick upon whom they lay their hands will recover" (Mk 16:17-20). This is what Jesus promised to those who believe, and it is to be taken seriously.

It is part of his covenant. The rules of the covenant are always within precise limits. In addition to great faith, it requires, first of all, the free choice of God and the free choice of ourselves to cooperate with God by believing in God. It requires on our part the willingness to do whatever God wants, no matter what anyone may think. Why are we surprised at God's willingness to do so much for us? "Is it possible that he who did not spare his own Son but handed him over for the sake of us all will not grant us all things besides?" (Rom 8:32). Why do we doubt God's commitment to us? "God so loved the world that he gave his only Son, that whoever believes in him may not die but may have eternal life" (Jn 3:16).

God loves the whole world so much that he wants to save the whole world, but the only ones he can save are those who believe in his Son and believe with all their heart, accept him totally as Lord in their lives. It is a covenant that excludes all "ifs and buts." It is God's total commitment, and it calls for the response of our total commitment. It is not something that mere sympathy for our suffering can change. It is not something that even the love of God will change. At Nazareth, "He could work no miracles . . . apart from curing a few who were sick by laying hands on them, so much did their lack of faith distress him" (Mk 6:5-6).

Spiritual, emotional, and physical healing have continued throughout the history of Christianity. They take place among people who believe deeply and take God at his given word. They accept completely the covenant that is Jesus. Is this personal commitment alive and real to us? Do we really believe that God wants us to invoke his commitment? Do we understand that Jesus wants to be used as our Mediator? Do we limit our faith by not taking seriouly certain parts of the New Testament? The covenant that is Jesus is an exchange of a life for a life in which Jesus gave his life that we may have life. If we believe unconditionally in Jesus and accept him totally as our God and our all, all our world, all our love, then his life becomes our life, his blood becomes our blood and his power enters into us as fully as the fullness of our faith. As is said in Proverbs, "My son, to my words be attentive; keep them within your heart; for they are life unto those who find them, to man's whole being they are health" (Prv 4:20-22). "He expelled the spirits by a simple command and cured all who were afflicted, thereby fulfilling what had been said through Isaiah the prophet: 'It was our infirmities he bore, our sufferings he endured' (Is 53:4)" (Mt 8:16-17).

Jesus completed his covenant work only with his ascension, when his Father confirmed and glorified his redemption of men. This completion of his work in heaven took it out of time and beyond time into the realm and the timelessness of eternity, where it goes on forever and ever. "Jesus because he remains forever, has a priesthood which does not pass away. Therefore, he is always able to save those who approach God through him, since he forever lives to make intercession for them" (Heb 7:24-25). Having entered into the timelessness of eternity, Jesus has not stopped for a moment being our redeemer and our covenant. Therefore, now, "Through him we have gained access through faith to the grace in which we now stand, and boast of our hope for the glory of God" (Rom 5:2). Moreover, every celebration of the Eucharist is a renewal of the covenant. "Every time, then, you eat this bread and drink this cup, you proclaim the death of the Lord until he comes!" (1 Cor 11:26). The covenant is in action on every altar. "As often as the sacrifice of the cross in which 'Christ, our passover, has been sacrificed' (1 Cor 5:7) is celebrated on an altar, the work of our redemption is carried on" (Vatican II, Constitution on the Church, no. 3).

The entire eighth chapter of Romans outlines in detail, point after point, the rich heritage which is ours because of the covenant relationship which we have through Christ our Lord. The final verses of that chapter speak our response to covenant love. They are a beautiful hymn of thanksgiving and praise.

> Who will separate us from the love of Christ? Trial, or distress, or persecution, or hunger, or nakedness, or danger, or the sword? As Scripture says, "For your sake we are being slain all the day long; we are looked upon as sheep to be slaughtered." Yet in all this we are more than conquerors because of him who has

loved us. For I am certain that neither death nor life, neither angels nor principalities, neither the present nor the future, nor powers, neither height nor depth, nor any other creature, will be able to separate us from the love of God that comes to us in Christ Jesus, our Lord. (Rom 8:35-39)

[1] The emphasis on covenant in this and subsequent chapters is due, positively, to its prominence in the Bible and, negatively, to the increasing reluctance to make personal commitments and abide by them. This difficulty is partly psychological and partly sociological. One's given word stands for one's self. If, through lack of authentic love from childhood, there is no sound self-respect, then there is no experience of the need or even of the possibility of standing by the commitment that expresses one's self. It is experienced as not "worth it" because the self is experienced as not "worth" much. Sociologically, a climate of irresponsibility aggravates the problem of commitment and fidelity for each person.

[2] The Pauline authorship of Hebrews is, of course, questioned by modern critics. Discussions of this kind are not within the scope of the present book.

CHAPTER 9

The Blood of the Covenant

Jesus is our covenant, and at a price, the price of giving his life, shedding his blood for us. This we know through the word of God that reaches back to the beginning of sacred history. One part of that history illumines another. As we have already seen, the sealing of a covenant with blood is recorded in the book of Exodus. The blood of the sacrificed victims stood for their life itself, and the sacrificial animals stood for the life of the Israelites who offered them. The altar stood for God in this covenant sealing. Moses splashed half of the sacrificial blood on the altar and then read aloud to the people the book of the covenant. The people answered, " 'All that the Lord has said, we will heed and do.' Then he took the blood and sprinkled it on the people, saying, 'This is the blood of the covenant which the Lord has made with you in accordance with all these words of his' " (Ex 24:6-8). The blood—part of it sprinkled on the altar, which represented God, and part sprinkled on the people—sealed God and his people in a blood pact. It meant the covenant partners shared a common life. They were one family.

There are other instances in the Old Testament in which blood is understood as the seal of the covenant. Thus in Exodus 4:24-25, when God was threatening Moses with death for having failed to circumcise his son, his wife Zipporah, by quickly circumcising him with a flint and offering God the blood of the circumcision, saved her husband's life. Again, blood has a role in the rite of consecration of priests (Ex 29:1-37; Lev 8:23-30). The blood of the ram of ordination (as opposed to the ram which had been made a burnt offering) was used as follows: part was splashed against the altar; part was smeared on the tip of the priest's right ear, on the thumb of his right hand, and on the great toe of his right foot (the ear that he should listen docilely to the word of God, the hand that he should be given to good works, the foot that he should walk in justice); and part, mixed with oil, was sprinkled over the whole person and vestments of the consecrated priest. Again, in Exodus 12:13, the blood of the Passover lamb, smeared on the doorposts and lintels of Israelite homes, protected the life of the first-born of their families from the angel of death: "The blood will mark the houses where you are. Seeing the blood, I will pass over you."

The one people of God moves in an unbroken line through symbol and preparation in the Old Testament into reality and fulfillment in the New Testament. Among the ancient Hebrews, as among practically every nation of antiquity, blood was regarded as sacred. Blood was the substance of animal life; life is conferred by God and is under his dominion; hence the eating of meat with the blood in it was prohibited. God reserved it to himself for his altar, as a sign through which men's sins would be expiated. Therefore, in the Expiation Day liturgy, the shedding of blood was the specific expiatory rite, since the blood stood for the sacrificial self-offering to the Most High God.

Passing quickly to the New Testament, we read:

> When Christ came as high priest of the good things which have come to be . . . he entered, not with the blood of goats and calves, but with his own blood, and achieved eternal redemption. For if the blood of goats and bulls and the sprinkling of a heifer's ashes can sanctify those who are defiled so that their flesh is cleansed, how much more will the blood of Christ, who through the eternal spirit offered himself up unblemished to God, cleanse our consciences from dead works to worship the living God! (Heb 9:11-14)

Unlike the sacrifices of the old covenant which prepared for it, Jesus' sacrifice is not local, limited, impersonal, external, and constantly to be repeated. The "much more" which the blood-sacrifice of Christ accomplished embraces four things: it is final, everlasting, efficacious, and infinitely superior. "On coming into this world, Jesus said: . . . 'As it is written of me in the head of the book, I have come to do your will, O God!' . . . By this 'will,' we have been sanctified through the offering of the body of Jesus Christ once for all . . . . By one offering he has forever perfected those who are being sanctified" (Heb 10:5,7,10,14). His sacrifice has the perfection of finality.

Secondly, it is everlasting. "He achieved an eternal redemption." And that means the eternal, timeless now of God's action. Jesus completed his redemptive action through his ascension into glory, and that took it out of time and inserted it into the continuity of eternity, where he goes on offering himself through the priest in every Mass and through every Christian in his heart. "Jesus is the one and eternal mediator between God and men, the man Jesus Christ, who gave himself a ransom for all" (1 Tm 2:5).

Thirdly, the blood of Christ offered for us accomplishes its purpose; it is efficacious. "Through his blood, God made him the means of expiation for all who believe" (Rom 3:25). We are redeemed. "God proves his love for us: that while we were still sinners, Christ died for us. Now that we have been justified by his blood, it is all the more certain that we shall be saved by him from God's wrath" (Rom 5:8-9). Surely, it is not what we have deserved but what God has gratuitously given. "It is in Christ and through his blood that we have been redeemed and our sins forgiven, so immeasurably generous is God's favor to us" (Eph 1:7-8). This sufficiency of Christ's primordial and eternal redemptive action does not, of course, exclude the association with his own suffering of the redemptive suffering he requires of each of his members. "In my own flesh I fill up what is lacking in the sufferings of Christ for the sake of his body, the church" (Col 1:24). Is there a true love that does not want to sacrifice, and sacrifice much, for the beloved?

Fourthly, Christ's sacrifice of his own blood was infinitely superior to all previous offerings. They had to be repeated endlessly both for the offerers and for all the people. But "Christ was offered up once to take away the sins of many" (Heb 9:28). His blood infinitely excels that of animals (Heb 9:13-14). He needed no man-made tabernacle or temple, for his own person was the temple of both the essential "will" and the Calvary offering (Heb 10:10; Lk 22:20). His offering was not temporary in its effect but eternal. "May the God of peace, who brought up from the dead Jesus our Lord, the great Shepherd of the sheep, by the blood of the eternal covenant, furnish you with all that is good, that you may do his will" (Heb 13:20-21). Moreover, his blood was innocent. "You were delivered from the futile way of life your fathers handed on to you, not by any diminishable sum of silver or gold, but by Christ's blood beyond all price: the blood of a spotless, unblemished lamb" (1 Pt 1:18-19). "It was fitting that we should have such a high priest: holy, innocent, undefiled, separated from sinners, higher than the heavens" (Heb 7:26).

The blood of the God-man Jesus effected at once two things—purification and sanctification:

> Brothers, since the blood of Jesus assures our entrance into the sanctuary by the new and living path he has opened up for us through the veil [the "veil" meaning his flesh], and since we have a great priest who is over the house of God, let us draw near in utter sincerity and absolute confidence, our hearts sprinkled clean from the evil which lay on our conscience and our bodies washed in pure water. (Heb 10:19-22)

Hence the blood of Christ, in taking away sin, at the same time unites us with God. Jesus is the bread that came down from heaven. Through his blood we ascend into heaven.

Moreover, the blood of Jesus freed the world of the fear of death as the end of everything and broke the power of the devil:

> "Here am I, and the children God has given me!" Now, since the children are men of blood and flesh, Jesus likewise had a full share in ours, that by his death he might rob the devil, the prince of death, of his power, and free those who through fear of death had been slaves their whole life long. (Heb 2:14-15)

The devil should not be feared for a power that is no longer his. We are certain of our own resurrection to glory if we are faithful to Christ. Death, now, is only the happy change which takes us into eternal peace, love, and joy; to our share in the glory of Christ's victory.

The positive effects in us of the covenant blood of Jesus are largely inseparable from the breaking of the devil's power. The death of the spirit was replaced by the inflowing of divine life and the indwelling of the Father, the Son, and the Holy Spirit. We are cleansed precisely by being filled with the innocence of grace. We no longer need fear the devil because we are armed with the power of Christ, we can plead with the merits of his precious blood in the face of whatever evil may threaten us, whatever trial may enter our lives; we are armed with Christ's power against all temptations, even the most distressing. Through Jesus we are united with God. "Now in Christ Jesus you who were once far off have been brought near through the blood of Christ. It is he who is our peace" (Eph 2:13-14). Through him we have the union and harmony of all things, and in him we can resolve all conflicts. "It pleased God to make absolute fullness reside in him and, by means of him, to reconcile everything in his person, both on earth and in the heavens, making peace through the blood of his cross" (Col 1:19-20).

This is the blood, together with water, that flowed from Christ's side, on the cross. "One of the soldiers thrust a lance into his side, and immediately blood and water flowed out" (Jn 19:34). Whether the explanation of this flow is supernatural or natural, the important things in John's testimony are: first, the unmistakable reality of Jesus' death is established; and, second, the prophecies concerning Jesus are fulfilled.

The first prophecy concerns the Passover Lamb. The soldiers did not break Jesus' legs (as they had done to the two who were crucified with him). Thus was the Scripture fulfilled: "Not a bone of him shall you break" (cf. Ps 34:21). The Old Testament Law about the lamb of the Passover sacrifice prescribed that it was to be "without blemish" (Ex 12:5). The second prophecy is from Zechariah, concerning the blessings ("a spirit of grace and petition") to be poured out on God's people through a mysterious, unknown sufferer like the Servant of the Lord in Is 52:13. "They shall look upon him whom they have pierced" (Zech 12:10; cf. Nm 21:9 and Rv 1:7).

This way of showing the spiritual meaning of an historical event is quite frequent in John. His symbols are open and flexible, capable of standing for many things. Hence also, from the Fathers to modern times, a special meaning has been given to the water from Christ's side (John Chrysostom, Augustine, Cyril of Alexandria, John Damascene, Thomas Aquinas), a meaning expressed by Pius XII:

> By reason of this symbol, which was not, indeed, unknown even to the ancient Fathers of the Church and ecclesiastical writers, the Common Doctor, as if re-echoing these same sentiments, writes: "Water flowed from Christ's side to wash us; blood to redeem us. Wherefore blood belongs to the Sacrament of the Eucharist, while water belongs to the Sacrament of Baptism. Yet this latter Sacrament derives its cleansing virtue from the power of Christ's blood." (*Haurietis Aquas*, n. 90)

But the meaning of the flow of water goes still deeper. Jesus visited Jerusalem for the Feast of Tabernacles, at which there was a rite of pouring out water to commemorate the miraculous flow of water from the rock which Moses struck in the desert (Ex 17:6). Perhaps Jesus referred to this Old Testament incident and to the commemorative rite when he

> stood up and cried out: "If anyone thirsts, let him come to me; let him drink who believes in me. Scripture has it: 'From within him rivers of living water shall flow.' " (Here he was referring to the Spirit, whom those that come to believe in him were to receive.) (Jn 7:37-39; cf. Is 12:2-3; Jn 4:10,14 and 19:34)

The promise of Jesus that water would flow from his side is to be taken in the light of the Old Testament prophecies that flowing water would be one of the signs of the Savior to come (cf. Is 12:3 and 44:3; Ez 36:25 and 47:1-12; Jl 4:18; Zec 13:1 and 14:8).

In John's Gospel, moreover, water is a sign of the Holy Spirit. "He was referring to the Spirit" (Jn 7:39). How is the water related to the blood? Because of the blood, the Spirit is given, poured out into the heart of the believer. The blood poured out in death releases a life that becomes the life of the redeemed. This takes John's message still further. While he has already made the Temple, the bronze serpent, and the manna stand for Jesus, he also sees Jesus, in the same sense as did St. Paul (cf. 1 Cor 10:4), as the spiritual rock from which Christians drink the outpouring of the Holy Spirit. As the power of God worked through the staff of Moses to make water flow from the rock to sustain the life of God's people (Ex 17:6), so the blood of Jesus serves to release the life-giving and life-sustaining water which is the Holy Spirit, our source of life and light. Everything that the Spirit brings—the Christian community of which he is the soul, the sacraments in which with Christ he acts, and all blessings and graces—everything comes from the sacrificial blood that flowed from Christ's side.

Although it is clear that in all activity outside the Godhead, Father, Son, and Holy Spirit act as one, theologians, out of regard for our human limitations, attribute certain activities to one of the Persons or the other: so, to the Holy Spirit is attributed the role of Sanctifier. St. Paul ascribes to the blood of Jesus all the graces of the Holy Spirit which St. John symbolizes by water. It is the Holy Spirit who, through the blood of Jesus, effects that union between God and man which is meant by the sprinkling upon altar and people of the blood of the covenant in Exodus 24 and which Jesus brings to full reality. Pius XII sums up this divine action as follows:

> Just as at the first moment of the Incarnation the Son of the Eternal Father, adorned with the fullness of the Holy Spirit the human nature which was substantially united to him, that it might be a fitting instrument of the Divinity in the sanguinary work of the redemption, so at the hour of his precious death he willed that his Church should be enriched with the abundant gifts of the Paraclete, in order that, in dispensing the divine fruits of the redemption, she might be, for the Incarnate Word, a powerful instrument that would never fail." (*Mystici Corporis*, n. 39)

Jesus came to the world because the Father sent him to pour out his blood, and through it to share with men the abundant gifts of the Spirit. He "came through water and blood" (1 Jn 5:6); i.e., first, he came to be baptized and receive his Father's witness as the beloved Son of his favor (Mt 3:17); and, secondly, he came to offer himself in a blood-sacrifice to accomplish the

Father's will. John, the first eyewitness to the outpouring of blood and water on Calvary, gave his testimony to confirm the faith of believers (Jn 19:35). In his First Epistle, again, he proclaims the witness value to believers of this flow of blood and water: through it the Holy Spirit, present at Christ's baptism, continues to give a witness to the work achieved through Christ by his presence in the Christian community. "It is the Spirit who testifies to this, and the Spirit is truth" (1 Jn 5:7; cf. Jn 15:26 and 19:34). "Thus there are three that testify, the Spirit and the water and the blood—and these three are of one accord . . . . Whoever believes in the Son of God possesses that testimony within his heart" (1 Jn 5:8,10). It would be in keeping with his symbolism to suppose that John is alluding here to baptism and the Eucharist and the continuing witness of water, blood, and the Spirit in the Christian community. All the sacraments derive their existence and efficacy from the death of Jesus. "The testimony is this: God gave us eternal life, and this life is in his Son. Whoever possesses the Son possesses life" (1 Jn 5:11-12).

The blood of Jesus poured out on Calvary won for mankind all the graces of the Christian life. This includes all the graces received by man from the beginning of sacred history and all those which are to be received until the end of time. The Eucharist applies those graces to us, in the degree that we desire them and are inwardly disposed to receive and to live by them. By shedding his blood on the cross Jesus gave us the Holy Spirit to be the soul of the Christian community. It is the Spirit, therefore, who, beginning with the baptism which initiates us into the Christian community, gives life, strengthens and enlightens us, and empowers us to carry forward the redemption effected by Christ.

We possess the life of God shared with us, a life that has been purchased for us by the blood of Jesus. "With your blood you purchased for God men of every race and tongue, of every people and nation" (Rv 5-9). This has been a deliverance, a liberation. That means a liberation from slavery, darkness, and alienation. "Everyone who lives in sin is the slave of sin"

(Jn 8:34). "If the Son frees you, you will really be free" (Jn 8:36). Sin is rejection of God, ignorance of God. "His command-ment is this: we are to believe in the name of his Son, Jesus Christ, and are to love one another" (1 Jn 3:23). "Were I to say I do not know him, I would be no better than you—a liar!" (Jn 8:55). Sin is a refusal to love. "The man who does not love is among the living dead" (1 Jn 3:14). Jesus liberates men from darkness and slavery. "If you live according to my teaching, you are truly my disciples; then you will know the truth, and the truth will make you free" (Jn 8:31-32). Redeemed Christians are free to know God and free to love him who is as the light of life. "I am the light of the world. No follower of mine shall ever walk in darkness; no, he shall possess the light of life" (Jn 8:12). And it is to be life in the Christian community. For Jesus was "to gather into one all the dispersed children of God" (Jn 11:52).

The victory of Christ the triumphant Savior that comes through so clearly and serenely in John means that the Christian's libera-tion from darkness puts the light of Christ into his faith, into his love for God and man, and into his whole moral life. In this way the blood of Jesus is linked with the light that he is to the world, "the light of life," and, therefore, with every aspect of Christian life. We are always "in the light," and especially in living that summary commandment of Jesus, "Love one another." So the redeeming blood is the reason for our unity in love and the power that alone makes it possible. "There is no greater love than this: to lay down one's life for one's friend" (Jn 15:13).

The ultimate union in love is our final glorification, body and spirit, in eternal life. The blood of Jesus together with his body feeds, strengtens, and intensifies the indwelling divine life in us that is our beginning of heaven, and so leads practicing and faithful believers on to their full glorification, the fullness of eternal life both for spirit and body. Moreover, the Savior's blood received as drink and his body as food establish an intimacy, an abiding union, with believers who partake of them. "He who feeds on my flesh and drinks my blood has life eternal, and I will raise him up on the last day. For my flesh is real food and my blood real drink. The man who feeds on my flesh and drinks my blood remains in me, and I in him" (Jn 6:54-56).

The apocalyptic figure of the immolated Lamb which is central in the book of Revelation expresses a profoundly rich teaching about Jesus and the redemption of man. Still bearing the marks of his sacrifice (Rv 5:6), the Lamb continues the constant linking up of Christ's death with his glory found in John's Gospel. Jesus, it will be recalled, referred to his death as his being "lifted up": "Just as Moses lifted up the serpent in the desert, so must the Son of Man be lifted up, that all who believe may have eternal life in him" (Jn 3:14-15). And again: "and I—once I am lifted up from earth—will draw all men to myself" (Jn 12:32). Death was his pathway to glory.

The Lamb is at once the Lamb slain, as Isaiah foretold (53:7), and the standing, triumphant One. His triumph is shown by all the pageantry surrounding him. It is also expressed by the seven horns, which are signs of power, and by the seven eyes (Zec 4:10), which are signs of God's all-knowing wisdom in governing the universe. Seven is a figure standing for fullness, perfection. The meaning of the eyes is further specified in Revelation 5:6 when it is said: "These eyes are the seven spirits of God, sent to all parts of the world." The spirits are the Holy Spirit who continues Christ's work. So the sacrificial Christ, pouring out his blood, is also the powerful, triumphant Redeemer through whom the Holy Spirit is sent into the whole world. And the heavenly hosts sing: "With your blood you purchased for God men of every race and tongue" (Rv 5:9).

Sharing the triumph of the victorious Lamb are the saints:

> After this I saw a great multitude which no man could number, out of all nations and tribes and peoples and tongues, standing before the throne and before the Lamb, clothed in white robes, and with palms in their hands. And they cried with a loud voice, saying: "Salvation belongs to our God Who sits upon the throne, and to the Lamb" . . . . "These are they who have come out of the great tribulation, and have washed their robes and made them white in the blood of the Lamb." (Rv 7:9,10,14)

The saints, therefore, are those who have reenacted in their own lives both the suffering and the triumph of Jesus. The Lamb whose blood won for them their cleansing in the water of baptism, which was for them the source of the divine life shared with them, completes his victory over darkness and death by leading them once again to living waters. "The Lamb on the throne will shepherd them. He will lead them to springs of life-giving water, and God will wipe away every tear from their eyes" (Rv 7:17). Moreover, the Lamb is now their light. "The city had no need of sun or moon, for the glory of God gave it light, and its lamp was the Lamb" (Rv 21:23). Finally, the Eucharist has its counterpart in the heavenly city, for the saints are "invited to the wedding feast of the Lamb" (Rv 19:9).

The beautiful hymns to the Lamb in Revelation were very probably songs of the primitive Christian community; if so, they were the kind of encouragement they needed under persecution. In the beginning they were more aware of what they had given up through losing the splendor of the Mosaic worship than they were of what they gained in their new way of life (Heb 10:25 and 13:10). They were ostracized and persecuted by their fellow Jews, and it was draining their faith (Heb 10:32-34). For Hebrews accustomed to see divine favor in material prosperity, such trials seemed a sign of God's abandoning them. They needed to know the meaning of suffering even unto blood for Jesus and after his example.

This is the encouragement that God has given to his faithful believers through the ages:

> The precious blood of my only-begotten Son destroyed death and darkness, confounded falsehood, and gave life and truth. For I give this blood and use it for the salvation and perfection of the man who disposes himself properly to receive it, for it gives life and adorns the soul with every grace, in proportion to the disposition and affection of him who receives it.[1]

---

[1] St. Catherine of Siena, *Dialogue* (Westminster, Md: Newman, 1943). p. 66.

CHAPTER 10

The Holy Spirit Empowers Us
to Live the Covenant

After Jesus had given his life for us and risen from the dead, he entered the final phase of his covenant relationship with his Father and with us. Entering into eternity, he lifted the covenant out of the order of time into the order and action of eternity. "Because he continues forever, he has an everlasting priesthood. Therefore he is able at all times to save those who come to God through him, since he lives always to make intercession for them" (Heb 7:25). He has never ceased to be our mediator, our covenant in continuous action. He has risen and yet he is still with us.

He is present to us in a very intimate way through the third person of the Trinity: "The Paraclete, the Holy Spirit[1] whom the Father will send in my name, will instruct you in everything, and remind you of all that I told you" (Jn 14:26). In Jn 7:37 we read:

> Now on the last, the great day of the feast, Jesus stood and cried out, saying, "If anyone thirst, let him come to me and drink. He who believes in me, as the Scripture says, 'From within him there shall flow rivers of living water.'" He said this, however, of the Spirit whom they who believed in him were to receive; for the Spirit had not yet been given, seeing that Jesus had not yet been glorified.

Through his unique, sacrificial death on Calvary and his resurrection in glory, Jesus gave birth to our life in the Spirit. He also gave birth to the Church on earth:

> To carry out the will of the Father, Christ inaugurated the kingdom of heaven on earth and revealed to us the mystery of the Father. By his obedience, he brought about redemption. The Church, or, in other words, the kingdom of Christ now present in mystery, grows visibly in the world through the power of God. This inauguration and this growth are both symbolized by the blood and water which flowed from the open side of the crucified Jesus (cf. Jn 19:34), and are foretold in the Lord's words concerning his death on the cross: "And I, once I am lifted up from earth, will draw all men to myself" (Jn 12:32). (Vatican II, Constitution on the Church, no. 3)

On the day of his resurrection Jesus gave the apostles the Holy Spirit:

> Jesus came and stood before them. "Peace be with you," he said. When he had said this, he showed them his hands and his side. At the sight of the Lord the disciples rejoiced. "Peace be with you," he said again. "As the Father has sent me, so I send you." Then he breathed on them and said, "Receive the Holy Spirit. If you forgive men's sins, they are forgiven them, if you hold them bound, they are held bound." (Jn 20:23)

The New Testament records two ascensions: the first (Jn 20:17) when Jesus, meeting Mary at the tomb, said: "Go to my brothers and tell them, 'I am ascending to my Father and your Father, to my God and your God' "; the second (Acts 1:9-11) when he rose visibly into heaven and a cloud took him out of the apostles' sight. With regard to this F.X. Durrwell writes:

> Père Benoit distinguishes two different streams of early tradition on the subject of the Ascension, one related to the visible ascension which gave the Apostles the certainty of their own experience of Christ's exaltation, the other to the essential Ascension which was identical with the glorification whereby Christ was lifted beyond this world into a heavenly existence. ("L'Ascension," *Revue Biblique* 56 [1949], pp. 161-203.)[2]

Commenting on the first ascension, he says:

> This return is not simply a physical change of place, identical with
> the visible ascension recorded in the Acts. The return is part of
> Christ's hour, and cannot be isolated from the mystery of his death
> as the visible ascension was. It completes a rising movement which
> began in the Passion, and it is simultaneous with the Resur-
> rection—which, according to Jn 10:17, is the end and object of
> his death. This ascent is a glorification, a change in his very being
> (17:5) which is above and beyond physical position. Christ receives
> it without any visible return to his heavenly dwelling; henceforth
> his existence is a marvel; his relationship with his disciples is on
> a new level (20:17); it is impossible not to believe in him (20:28),
> which is a characteristic of his glorified state (17:2-4); he gives
> them the Holy Spirit (20:22) whom he would not be free to give,
> according to 7:39, till after he was glorified, and according to 15:26,
> until he had returned to his Father. This idea of his return is vital
> to the fourth gospel; had it been effected by the visible ascension,
> St. John would hardly have omitted to record it.[3]

During forty days after his resurrection Jesus appeared often
to his apostles, instructing them and confirming their faith. Just
before his final, visible ascension into heaven, he told them
not to leave Jerusalem, but to wait there—Jerusalem, the holy
city, the city central to the whole of salvation history, the covenant city towards which the Old Testament moved forward,
and out of which was to begin the full activity of the Church
to which he gave life on Calvary. "Wait," he said, "for the
fulfillment of my Father's promise, of which you have heard
me speak . . . . John baptized with water, but within a few days
you will be baptized with the Holy Spirit" (Acts 1:4-5).

At Pentecost the Holy Spirit, already given as the life of the
Church, was manifested with power:

> When the days of Pentecost were drawing to a close, they were
> all together in one place. And suddenly there came a sound from
> heaven, as of a violent wind coming, and it filled the whole house
> where they were sitting. And there appeared to them parted
> tongues of fire, which settled upon each of them. And they were
> all filled with the Holy Spirit. They began to express themselves

in foreign tongues and make bold proclamations as the Spirit prompted them. Staying in Jerusalem at the time were devout Jews of every nation under heaven. These heard the sound, and assembled in a large crowd. They were much confused because each one heard these men speaking in his own language. The whole occurrence astonished them . . . . They were dumbfounded, and could make nothing at all of what had happened. "What does this mean?" they asked one another, while a few remarked with a sneer, "They have had too much new wine!" (Acts 2:2-7, 12-13).

On that day, the Church, already born out of Christ's side, entered into its full, mature activity, with Peter already acting as its head and speaking in its name:

Peter, who stood up with the Eleven, raised his voice and addressed them: "You who are Jews, indeed all of you staying in Jerusalem! Listen to what I have to say. You must realize that these men are not drunk, as you seem to think. It is only nine in the morning! No, it is what Joel the prophet spoke of: It shall come to pass in the last days, says God" (Acts 2:14-17).

"In the last days": day here is meant in the sense given it by St. Paul, that one final "day" of salvation which began with Christ and extends to the end of time: "Now is the day of salvation" (2 Cor 6:12). The phenomenon they were witnessing, Peter was explaining, this outpouring of the Holy Spirit, was a manifestation with power of an event already taking place; they should have expected it, for it was what the prophet Joel had prophesied: "I will pour out a portion of my Spirit upon all mankind: Your sons and daughters shall prophesy, your young men shall see visions and your old men shall dream dreams. Yes, even on my servants and handmaids I will pour out a portion of my Spirit in those days, and they shall prophesy" (Acts 2:17-18, Jl 3:1-5). Contrary to the standards of their religious culture and to all their expectations, God made no distinctions among men, all were to be equal in his sight. All were to be filled with the outpouring of the Holy Spirit irrespective of their status in society, even slaves who counted as nothing, even women, who were without position in the culture of the day. Now for the first time, with the coming of Christ, all are equal before God. All believers receive the Holy Spirit, and with it may be gifted with visions, with the power to speak in tongues and prophesy.

This revelation is part of the teaching of Our Lord contained in the parable of the wise and foolish virgins. Be alert, he said, for the Son of Man would come when they least expected it. He was referring not merely to the final coming but to the ways in which he would manifest himself through his Holy Spirit.

The Holy Spirit is ever active in helping us to live our covenant relationship with God. From the beginning of our Christian existence he is the source of our new life. "No one can enter into God's kingdom without being begotten of water and Spirit" (Jn 3:5). Through him, in Christ, we are adopted as God's children. "The proof that you are sons is the fact that God has sent forth into our hearts the spirit of his Son which cries out "Aba!" ("Father!") (Gal 4:6). Through him we are coheirs with Christ of eternal life. "The Spirit himself gives witness with our spirit that we are children of God. But if we are children, we are heirs as well: heirs of God, heirs with Christ, if only we suffer with him so as to be glorified with him" (Rom 8:16-17).

We hold the Holy Spirit in the sacred temple of our hearts. "Are you not aware that you are the temple of God, and the Spirit of God dwells in you?" (1 Cor 3:16). "Your body is a temple of the Holy Spirit, who is within—the Spirit you have received from God. You are not your own. You have been purchased, and at a price. So glorify God in your bodies" (1 Cor 6:19-20).

He is the source of our sanctification. "It is in the spirit that we eagerly await the justification we hope for, and only faith can yield it . . . faith, which expresses itself through love . . . You should live in accord with the spirit" (Gal 5:5, 16). Through him we learn the truth that leads to life. "Being the Spirit of truth, he will guide you to all truth" (Jn 16:13). "Of this wisdom it is written: 'Eye has not seen, ear has not heard, nor has it so much as dawned on man what God has prepared for those who love him.' Yet God has revealed this wisdom to us through the Spirit. The Spirit scrutinizes all matters, even the deep things of God" (1 Cor 2:9-10). He shows us Jesus. Through him we experience Jesus.

From the Holy Spirit we receive love as a gift. "The love of God has been poured out in our hearts through the Holy Spirit who has been given us" (Rom 5:5). Through him we serve our brothers and sisters in Christ. "There are different gifts but the same Spirit; there are different ministries but the same Lord. To each person the manifestation of the Spirit is given for the common good" (1 Cor 12:4-5, 7).

It is the Holy Spirit who unites us in deep fellowship in the heart of our being. "It was in one Spirit that all of us, whether Jew or Greek, slave or free, were baptized into one body. All of us have been given to drink of the one Spirit. If one member suffers, all the members suffer with it; if one member is honored, all the members share its joy" (1 Cor 12:13,26). "Make every effort to preserve the unity which has the Spirit as its origin and peace as its binding force. There is but one body and one Spirit, just as there is but one hope given all of you by your call. There is one Lord, one faith, one baptism; one God and Father of all, who is over all, and works through all, and is in all" (Eph 4:3-6).

Through the Holy Spirit we receive the power and conviction to witness to Christ and his redeeming action. "You will receive power when the Holy Spirit comes down on you; then you are to be my witnesses in Jerusalem, throughout Judea and Samaria, yes, even to the ends of the earth" (Acts 1:8).

The Holy Spirit teaches us how to pray and even intercedes for us. "The Spirit too helps us in our weakness, for we do not know how to pray as we ought; but the Spirit himself makes intercession for us with groanings that cannot be expressed in speech" (Rom 8:26).

It has been common to think of the gifts of the Holy Spirit as they have been outlined in the Old Testament (cf. Is 11:2-3). This approach has the sanction of traditional theology, notably in the detailed development of St. Thomas Aquinas and in John of St. Thomas. As Aquinas developed these gifts, they are given to perfect the virtues, directly for the benefit of the individual.

God's word, of course, does not contradict itself; it only expresses
its one message more and more clearly. The Old Testament
emphasizes the solidarity of God's people in all things. Therefore, indirectly, the gifts of the Spirit are also for the common
good.

In First Corinthians, chapter 12, nine specific gifts of the Holy
Spirit are listed. These are to be taken in the context of Peter's
speech on Pentecost quoted above (Acts 2:16-17): the true sense
of Joel's prophecy is that the outpouring of the Holy Spirit was
to be upon everyone without distinction and for the common
good.

The beautiful homily on charity of First Corinthians, chapter
13, can be understood only within the context of chapters 12
and 14. St. Paul was dealing with a single problem: the main
point of his discourse is that the gifts are meant to serve the
common good:

> The Spirit guides the Church into the fullness of truth (cf. Jn 16:13)
> and gives her a unity of fellowship and service. He furnishes and
> directs her with various gifts, both hierarchical and charismatic,
> and adorns her with the fruits of his grace (cf. Eph 4:11-12; 1
> Cor 12:4; Gal 5:22). (Vatican II, Constitution on the Church, no. 4)

These gifts are the heritage of believers. They are part of the
covenant between God and men that is in the person of Christ
Jesus. It belongs to the role of the Holy Spirit to show us Jesus,
to give us an experience of Jesus as truly our covenant and
the source of all our confidence and our strength. Faith comes
by hearing. So if there is to be faith in the gifts of the Holy
Spirit, they have to be preached. For otherwise, how can they
serve the common good? They must be taught along with the
whole of Mark 16 and Acts 2. Only with a living faith in the
entire New Testament can Christians attain and give witness
to the full fruits of the Spirit. "The fruit of the spirit is love,
joy, peace, patient endurance, kindness, generosity, faith, mildness and chastity" (Gal 5:22-23).

Fortunately there is a tendency to delay the sacrament of confirmation until adolescence. This permits the natural maturing,
the deeper understanding, and the spiritual preparation which

are necessary for what is called by John the Baptist and by Jesus himself "baptism with the Holy Spirit." Of course, from the moment of baptism we are given the divine life and are indwelt by the divine persons; the Spirit is with us and operative in us. But there is a special mode of the Spirit's presence which comes as something new in the Christian's experience. Whether through the sacrament of confirmation or through some special preparation later in life and the special prayers of Spirit-filled persons, suddenly the Christian has an awareness of the Holy Spirit, his power and his gifts, by which he feels renewed and re-created from within. Spiritual writers sometimes refer to this as the baptism of the Holy Spirit.

This experience is to judged by its fruits. Quite commonly it results in a transformation of life marked by the various fruits of the Spirit, especially deep inner peace and an outgoing love for others, and also by some of the gifts. There is normally a new delight and new understanding in reading the Bible. Jesus comes alive as a person in the New Testament. The Acts of the Apostles take on new meaning. Personal prayer is transformed and corporate worship is experienced with a new depth of meaning.

If we are to respond fully to the covenant that is Jesus, we must be led by the promptings of the Holy Spirit even into danger, as Jesus was: "Then Jesus was led into the desert by the Spirit to be tempted by the devil" (Mt 4:1). We do not know what our trials may be. Our Lord has warned us that we may have to testify to our faith under persecution: "If the world hates you, know that it has hated me before you . . . . No servant is greater than his master. If they have persecuted me, they will persecute you also" (Jn 15:18,20). But whatever trials come, we have the promise that the Holy Spirit, the Comforter, will be with us.

But apart from the crises of life, our loyalty to Christ should make us want to live as becomes our status, dignity, and power as children of God. "All who are led by the Spirit of God are sons of God" (Rom 8:14). We must very realistically face the tendencies within ourselves which cloud our spiritual vision and make us insensitive to the Spirit's promptings. It has been the experience of the saints, and it is the experience of many Spirit-filled persons, that when an impulse is felt to do or say something which will benefit another, or the Christian community, or even ourselves, but it is something which will require a little courage, fear must first be overcome. But if there is no reason against our doing it, after we have examined it in the light of sound Christian teaching and various factors in our own circumstances, we should go ahead. This docility to good impulses should be encouraged, because so much good is blocked by timidity and false prudence. Indeed, the notion that the safer course is necessarily the surer is part of the mystery of evil. Why not take God at his word? We shall find that if we trust God and go ahead, extraordinary things are likely to happen—"little miracles," some like to call them. Why is it so easy for us to be weighed down by the evil in the world, and so difficult for us to look around us and see how much good Christ is daily accomplishing? Already, living with the risen life of Christ, we have the power within us to accomplish our destiny. "If the Spirit of him who raised Jesus from the dead dwells in you, then he who raised Christ from the dead will bring your mortal bodies to life also, through his Spirit dwelling in you" (Rom 8:11).

---

[1] For the biblical concept of Spirit cf. J. L. McKenzie, *Dictionary of the Bible* (Milwaukee: Bruce, 1965), pp. 842-845; also *Jerome Biblical Commentary* (Englewood Cliffs, N.J.: Prentice-Hall, 1969), Vol. II, *The New Testament*, pp. 425,456.

[2] *The Resurrection* (New York: Sheed and Ward, 1960), p. 39, note 9.

[3] Ibid., p. 38.

III

Prayerful

CHAPTER 11

Our Natural Need to Pray

In an earlier chapter we have dealt with certain elements in the environment which threaten our personality development as well as our immediate peace and happiness. What is more important, these same elements hinder our relationship and our integration with our entire environment, indeed with the whole of reality. As a consequence they intimately affect our relationship with God. The question each of us must ask himself is, Do I have control of my life? Do I have enough understanding of the surroundings which encompass my life to maintain a balance between integrating myself with them and detaching myself from them—placing myself at sufficient distance to permit my survival as a free and intelligent person to whose destiny this world is not an end it itself but a means?

One of the matters for concern is precisely something that is good in itself but which seems to be developing beyond our human control—namely, the technology which has brought us such great economic and cultural benefits. Do we, for example, know the right use of the abundance of goods, of drugs and alcohol, of our expanded opportunities for leisure and recreation—of that fascinating entertainer and teacher that is called television? Where do we stand in regard to our environment and its daily impact on us?

Given the pace of modern life, the individual undergoing pressures from all directions—work, social obligations, the problems of family life, the sheer physical and nervous strain of getting from one place to another in our crowded cities—often feels overwhelmed by the mere business of living. There seems to be no time to experience oneself as a human person with all the richness and mysterious depths of our being, no time to relate calmly with others. There is serious danger that we shall not take the time to relate to God, who is the center and the meaning of the little universe around us. If this is what is happening to us, then we are leading a life that is unrealistic, fragmented, piecemeal, out of focus. Do we recognize ourselves in this picture?

Another factor which contributes to our problem of adjustment to our environment is the change in religious culture which has come in our age. The thoughtful individual has the problem of trying to analyze the traditions and beliefs of the past and to integrate what is perennially true and viable with the valid trends in a rapidly changing social environment. He must learn to distinguish between what is, practically speaking, beyond human control and what can be regulated by patient effort, so that development may be organic, and from within. In any event, it is the task of maturity to become aware of the forces at work in our environment and to adapt ourselves to the changes which can be orientated towards God. And we shall do this so that our manner of dealing with others will be an expression of everything that is good in the mainstream of our society; so that we can bring our lives into harmony with the whole reality about us and not be confused, fragmented, alienated from others.

Our need for others, if our development as persons is to be normal, is paralleled by a need for privacy. There is no doubt whatever that our human nature absolutely demands a certain amount of solitude in which one can grow as a human being with the riches of personality which are the exclusive characteristic of each distinct person. Only thus can the capacity to communicate effectively with others develop; only thus can the capacity for meditation and affective prayer develop which is indispensable to our progress in maturity.

The greatest difficulties in maintaining our essential privacy come from a category of persons we shall call the intruders. There are people who have a compulsive tendency to meddle with the lives of others. Everything other people do seems to be the object of morbid curiosity on their part. Suppose a neighbor has gone away; the intruder is full of speculation as to his motive for going, where he went and for how long. The whole thing seems to this keeper of his brother most suspicious. He is himself very inventive of immoral explanations for events, for he takes a pessimistic view of human virtue. Sometimes he will be the source of rumors which he eventually comes to believe.

Perhaps these intruders' tendency to meddle continuously in matters that do not concern them is largely due to a failure to be at home with themselves. They compulsively violate the privacy of others because they have no positive, constructive satisfaction of the basic needs for self-identity, security, and intellectual stimulation. The intruder feels bored with himself and everything else, lonely, empty, drifting, with no confidence in his capacity to make his life stimulating and meaningful. He feels incapable of commiting himself to others—friends or family—to his work, or to God.

There are, of course, many other kinds of people whose intrusion on our privacy is more innocent. We have all suffered from the well-intentioned person who would give us more advice than we need; psychologically aggressive by nature, he unconsciously tries to form everyone else according to his compulsive mold. Indeed, intruders are as various as human nature itself.

In any community of authentic persons uneasiness develops if privacy is intruded upon—if there is someone around who takes an inordinate interest in what we are doing, who our friends are, what our family relations are like, how our inner life is developing. Therefore each group—familial, neighborhood, religious, etc.—must have the defense of privacy built into its life style. If such structures do not exist, the tensions which develop are likely to produce irritability, depression, fatigue, and even physical ailments such as high blood pressure and ulcers. Inner peace is lost and recollection and prayer are difficult. All this naturally diminishes the energy which should be dedicated to a full participation in the affairs of the community and hinders the spirit of community itself. It also takes its toll of the personal growth both of the intruders and of their victims. Experience indicates that if there is an attempt to live without arrangements for the protection of privacy, implicit structures take their place which are a desperate reaction against invasion.

The need of privacy is intimately related to the need of peace in order to experience our own being and God. This basic need is threatened by a tendency to activism—to excessive and continuous activity with no pause for reflection. Fortunately, there has been increasing dialogue devoted to the object of analyzing activities, their motives and what they achieve. One conclusion that is already emerging is the absolute necessity of taking time for reflection and prayer.

Similar conclusions with regard to the necessity man has for sufficient repose to experience his own being are being reached in widely different quarters. Charles Reich writes:

> Consciousness is profoundly affected simply by the din and over-stimulation of our society. It is pounded, battered, strained, exhausted and inevitably, dulled . . . . Encounters with people are so many, so brutish and impersonal, so fleeting and so harrowing that consciousness must be desensitized to reduce the pain . . . . There is an effort to restore, protect and foster human consciousness . . . to restore man's awareness of himself, of other people, of nature, of his own life.[1]

Industrial research teams, management teams, and corporation boards are moving away from the centers of manufacturing and commercial activity and setting up their main offices and research centers somewhere in the country, often literally in the woods. Here they find that they can think more clearly, plan better, direct more rationally the work of manufacturing and distribution that is carried on in the great industrial and urban centers. Research and management teams become, in a sense, people apart.

Scholars, musicians, and artists have always recognized this need to seek a certain undisturbed privacy in order to pull themselves together, organize themselves and their thoughts, and concentrate on creative work.

But intellectual endeavors apart, we all need to get away at times, away from the pressures, the worries, the problems calling for decision which pull us in many directions at once. We need to withdraw to think out, digest, and assimilate personal experiences and find rest for the body and peace for mind and heart. If we deny ourselves this withdrawal for too long, others will suffer for it in terms of strained human relations. No one can afford to play the inexhaustible God.

Parents should remember this. The mother of a family feels pulled apart by the incessant demands of the distinctive personalities of her children—no two of them alike. She also feels worn out from what seems to be their inexhaustible energy.

In children, activity is the way of growing. From the moment the baby begins to kick its little legs and throw its arms around and toss its head, movement is the process of growth. Play is a child's work. It is his way of development. He needs to move about, see, learn, explore, experience many things, because through such activity the uncertain personality is discovering itself in relation to a very diverse and very rich world. But children, too, need times of quiet, of being happy "just to be." That is often one of the most difficult things for parents to arrange, and yet it is very necessary. The period set aside for the afternoon nap can be such a time, even if the child does not fall asleep. Then there are those times of just resting in the arms of the father or mother who loves them. In that resting they experience themselves.

Sometimes the more altruistic and spiritual the goals are which we have set for ourselves or others have set for us, the greater the danger that we shall try to play the little god or goddess who can keep on going indefinitely without rest. But if we fail to exercise discretion in this matter, we shall find the vision of the goals themselves becoming less clear. At the same time we shall find ourselves losing our grasp on our own motivation, and our personal resources failing. Our spiritual nature becomes subordinated to a thing: work and more work. The result is that we are not at liberty to attend to God, who is the center and focus of all reality and all truth. So often our loss of hope is traceable to this cause.

The problem of so ordering our work and other activities as to make time for what is really essential to human living must be solved by each of us individually, and the solution will be as distinctive as the individual person, his way of life and his attitudes towards himself, towards others, and towards God. Sooner or later everyone has to decide what amount of the time and energy he is expending is directed towards a goal which is the right one for him personally. We must ask ourselves whether we are in any sense trying to live up to a false self-image. How much of our running hither and yon is a way of trying to escape from facing ourselves, re-evaluating our activities, and taking the necessary security risk of leaving off part of what we are doing for the sake of giving a new direction to life?

More than quiet is needed for such profound self-searching, we must have leisure; and creating this necessary leisure, which is our first step, may well be very difficult for some people. But in doing so we shall already have recognized a natural need for experiencing ourselves and seen it as of greater value than what must be sacrificed to make it possible. As a result we shall discover in ourselves a new openness to truth and to being. Our very decision has been a reassertion of the rational over the purely instinctive, of the true over the false; and therefore an affirmation of the authentic human person we search for in prayer and ultimately find "hidden in obscurity and 'nothingness,' at the center where we are in direct dependence on God . . . . My true self lies hidden in God's call to my freedom and my response to him." [2] The decision to make way for prayer is both an exercise of freedom and a growth in freedom. Intelligence has guided freedom to choose the good of the whole person over the desires of an element in the person which is partial and out of order.

This reordering of our lives is a necessary approach to meeting God, who is all truth and all reality, in prayer. The achievement of this orientation towards God is every man's vocation, and so we should not feel guilty about the things which must be sacrificed to it, even though they are in themselves good things. When our lives are directed towards God there is room in them for everything we should do according to his will. Suppose what must be sacrificed is some little immediate service to others: we may be confident that from our time spent with God we shall return capable of ministering more truly to others' needs because we are more truthfully, firmly, and peacefully related to ourselves, to God, and to our fellow men. With everything in better focus it is more likely that we shall serve the real needs of others rather than their misguided desires—or even our own self-image or our defensive need to "feel good" by playing the benefactor. In prayer we will be better able to see the self-image we have been trying to cultivate for what it is and learn that God values us for ourselves and not for any of the things we are doing.

Our responsibility for one another includes the recognition of everyone's natural need to pray; we should help one another achieve the reordering of our lives which makes prayer possible. There is the matter of availability to one another: this at times will require sensitive decisions of prudence, especially in view of the great need a person may have, in a moment of discouragement or depression, just to have someone who cares enough to really listen. For such decisions there can be no set rules. They call for a sensitive blend of love, truth, and wise perception. The obvious is not always the real, nor is the deeply hidden necessarily a mere shadow. Somehow heart must speak to heart, and both hearts must be courageously responsive to the Holy Spirit.

Such a need for perceptiveness emphasizes the necessity of habitual prayer, where God teaches us through his word and through speaking in our hearts that his ways are not our ways. In prayer we experience that unhurried reflection which puts at a sufficient distance the preoccupations that get things out of focus, and we are able to open our being to the lights that come to us through self-understanding, through other people and things, and from God. It is, once again, each man's personal decision to be so open and ready that God can speak to him and re-orientate his life. Nobody can make that decision for him, nor can anyone else reap its fruits, except in the sense that the peace God gives him diffuses itself. It is a personal need and a personal enrichment.

Reordering our thinking is difficult enough. Still more complex is the reordering of feeling. A great love can throw everything else out of perspective; and if this has happened, withdrawal from the stimulation of this inordinate affection is essential until perspective is restored. The length of time and the degree of withdrawal will be determined by the nature and intensity of the love. But even when such distancing has been achieved that we can reflect calmly and let the light of reason bring persons and responsibilities into focus, it takes great courage to keep on looking clearly at our situation, and greater courage still to follow through on the course which truth sets before us. We are so much inclined to take fright and retreat from the unwelcome light, whether by way of declaring ourselves incapable of surrendering the love or by way of rejecting or distorting the light.

The love need not be for a person: it may be enthusiasm for a project, an idea, a movement, or a career. In any case, whether to see the light or to follow it, man needs more than his own powers to make the decision and carry it to an ordered conclusion. He needs the strength which comes from prayer. He needs the God he encounters in prayer, the all-powerful God who can help him to do what he is unable to do by himself.

More commonly, the feeling out of control is negative, whether in regard to oneself, to others, or to God. Fear, for instance: generally originating in childhood, deepseated and hidden, it may call for professional counseling. But most of our fears do not amount to deep psychological disturbances, and even though hidden they can yield to prayer, both indirectly and directly. The first step in healing is taken when such a person conquers his guilt feelings about relinquishing some activity or work for the sake of giving time to prayer. In prayer itself, rightly orientated, we encounter a God of mercy and love to whose goodness we can yield ourselves with confidence. Prayer is normally a constant reasserting of positive emotions over the negative, and therefore a constant process of healing. All along, God is gently at work giving his love as a gift through the Holy Spirit and thus affirming and strengthening all right personal values and all personal efforts to grow in love. We must be aware, of

course, of the extent to which our feelings seem to be recorded
in the cortex of the brain, and complete healing would therefore
be something of a physical miracle. But if God wants to
accomplish that also, he can easily do it; nothing is hard for
him. The only hard part is ours—achieving the faith God asks
for the working of miracles.

Whatever the personal need may be that calls us to the
encounter with God in prayer, we must anticipate changes,
upsets, failures and defeats, for they are normal to life. We
all receive blows, and at one time we can take them in stride
without harmful disturbance to a wholesome attitude about ourselves, about others, or about God. At other times they may
threaten to shatter us. In either case our best recourse is prayer.
We should think our situation through in the full awareness
that God is in control of his world and that he has committed
himself to our protection in the covenant he made in Jesus.
So nothing can happen to us which is beyond God's repair.
Even the most distressing and devastating events—say, the
death of a loved one, or even multiple deaths in our family
owing to some disaster—while they may try one's faith to the
limit at which the darkness of grief and rebellion seem to shut
out all light, do not separate us from God. He hears our cries
of despair and knows that what looks like rebellion is only a
sign of the intensity of our inner suffering. All the while, he
is inwardly healing the raw wound and strengthening and
purifying our faith and love.

Only God can say, "I am who am"; for he is the only necessary
being. He, the infinite God, is the only sufficient reason why
an infinite God should act. All the greater the mystery, then,
of his love for us, contingent beings who depend upon him
for our existence from moment to moment; who receive from
him all that we have and are. From him we receive our worth,
and he wants us to value and love the precious being he put
in us. Only when we experience through prayer that God loves
us for what we are can we rightly accept ourselves and rightly
serve God and our fellow men. God wants us to be happy
in the person he made us to be, a person he chooses as the
sanctuary of his indwelling presence. He wants us to be happy

in the richness of being he placed in us and to serve him and other men out of the richness of that being. The greater the depth and complexity of a personality, the more it needs to be focused, concentrated, unified, and coordinated through prayer in which God becomes the infinite meaning of everything.

Brought into focus and confirmed in peace through prayer to our God and meditation on what Jesus did for us and how he did it, we shall be less inclined to take ourselves too seriously or overestimate ourselves, i.e. less inclined to pride. We shall be peacefully content to stay within our limitations and try to do well what God gives us to do at the moment. While we shall keep ourselves alert to world needs with a world-embracing vision and love, we shall not try to take on the world. Rather, we shall humbly keep to the simple truth of what we are, of what we can do, well aware that we are each a part of the truth and power that God shares with men and that millions of others also are sharing and carrying on the work of the redemption at the same moment with us.

As will be explained later, this natural need to pray can at times be satisfied through personal private prayer. At other times, it can best be satisfied through praying together with people who are united in a deep affective warmth and mutual concern.

[1] *The Greening of America* (New York: Random House, 1970), pp. 253–254.

[2] Thomas Merton, *Contemplative Prayer* (New York: Herder and Herder, 1969), pp. 87, 84.

CHAPTER 12

Covenant Prayer Is Prophetic Prayer

Jesus is the God-man who is our covenant. He is God's supreme message to us. Through him we have sure access to the Father's heart. Accepting his fidelity to his promise, we know that our prayer offered through Jesus becomes covenant prayer. We know that covenant prayer is also prophetic prayer, for it at once proclaims the truth of God and points forward to the certain answer God will give in his own time and way.

In the Old Testament, a prophecy had to be accepted and believed before it would be fulfilled. Abraham accepted the prophecy of God that he would be the father of a great nation, and on that promise he left home and country and set out for an unknown land. He went on believing even when God asked him to sacrifice his only and beloved son. "Hoping against hope, Abraham believed, and so became the father of many nations, just as it was once told him" (Rom 4:18).

In Egypt, God's people accepted the word of God that their sons would be spared if they prepared the Passover lamb and sprinkled his blood on the door posts. Their first-born sons were saved, and the Passover lamb became the figure of our Savior.

Mary accepted the word of the Lord that she would be with child and become the mother of the most high God, even though she was not yet married. When Elizabeth praised her for trusting in the Lord—"Blest is she who trusted that the Lord's words to her would be fulfilled" (Lk 1:45)—Mary poured out her Magnificat, prophetic prayer that at once proclaimed what God was, what he had done for his people, and the extension of God's promise to Abraham's "descendants forever." This point we will enlarge upon later.

When Jesus came to John for baptism and John protested to Jesus, "I should be baptized by you, yet you come to me!", Jesus answered: "Give in for now. We must do this if we would fulfill all of God's demands." So John gave in. After Jesus was baptized, he came directly out of the water. Suddenly the sky opened and he saw the Spirit of God descend like a dove and hover over him. With that, a voice from the heavens said, "This is my beloved son. My favor rests on him" (Mt 3:14-17). Then John recognized Jesus as the Messiah.

At the raising of Lazarus, Martha protested that Lazarus was so long dead there would be a stench if they opened the tomb. Jesus said, "Did I not assure you that if you believed, you would see the glory of God displayed?" (Jn 11:40).

The summary of prophetic prayer is in John's first Epistle: "Since we know that he hears us whenever we ask, we know that what we ask him for is ours" (1 Jn 5:15). We know that he gives us whatever we ask from him. We know this beforehand. So our prayer becomes at once a proclaiming of God's power and fidelity and an assurance, a foretelling, of an answer.

Therefore, even as we pray, we must believe beforehand that our prayer is answered. We have every reason to believe and pray this prophetic way. The whole history of salvation shows God's power and desire to save men and his fidelity to his word. Jesus himself strongly and repeatedly (Mt 18:19; Jn 15:16 and 16:23) urged us to absolute confidence in obtaining anything we ask through him. He means for us to take him seriously and believe absolutely, and at the moment of praying, that every prayer is answered.

We should really expect this because Christ is our covenant and has given us his word that the Father will give us anything we ask in his name. He has committed the Father to answer us. He has given us his power (Jn 14:12), his Holy Spirit (Jn

14:26), his peace (Jn 15:15), and his joy (Jn 15:11). He has given us unity (Jn 17:22-23). He wants us to be vitally functioning Christians and active witnesses to his redemptive work and to his covenant commitment. He wants to answer our prayers. He wants us to be his friends, to be happy and at peace, to accept his Holy Spirit and put God's power into action. This is God's commitment. He has committed himself to us, and we should accept his commitment, take him seriously and respond in kind.

Our commitment is to believe in him and to do his will. We cannot want anything else. Therefore, we pray as he wants us to pray. Through our prophetic prayer, taking the answer for granted, knowing the answer ahead of time, we claim the answer. We claim the fulfillment of what we ask for by the covenant that Jesus is between the Father and ourselves. And we claim it by the blood of Jesus that he told us sealed this covenant. This is the reason we call upon his blood. It is by the blood of Jesus that this covenant is sealed and God has made his commitment. As blood sealed the covenant between God and his people, given through Moses, so the new and everlasting covenant is sealed by the infinitely more precious blood of Jesus. "This is the chalice of my blood, the blood of the new and everlasting covenant." In every Mass we renew this covenant. So by his blood we claim this covenant and the commitment of God to fulfill it. By our prophetic prayer we remind God of his covenant, of his commitment; we, as it were, nail the promises of God on the doorposts of heaven so that he cannot forget them or ignore them. Hence we can say that covenant prayer is prophetic prayer. We are proclaiming the message of God, the commitment of God, and the fidelity of God to his given word, through Jesus our Savior. And our prayer becomes the sign, the foretelling, of the answer that God is giving.

This confidence in prayer is consistent with the very nature of God, because in God there is no time, neither past, present, nor future. He sees both our prayer and our answer in one eternal now. The answer is not something that God has to calculate and add up and make a decision about in the future. In

God the future is present in the eternal now. He has always known our petition as well as its fulfillment.

Moreover, we have complete confidence that God is totally in control of his world. Everything is easy for him. There is nothing hard for God. There is nothing that can prevent him from doing what he wills and as he wills. By his very nature, God wills only our good, never anything else. On our part, when we pray sincerely, we can ask only for what is good and good for us, for others, or for the Christian community. We do not ask for what is to anyone's harm—not consciously. Besides, we take for granted that what we ask for is already what he wills for our good. We are not trying to change God's mind but only to fulfill the conditions he made for being heard. He told us to ask:

> Ask, and you will receive. Seek, and you will find. Knock, and it will be opened to you. The one who asks, receives. The one who seeks, finds. The one who knocks, enters. Would one of you hand his son a stone when he asks for a loaf, or a poisonous snake when he asks for a fish? If you, with all your sins, know how to give your children what is good, how much more will your heavenly Father give good things to anyone who asks him? (Mt 7:7-11)

This is God's commitment to us. Therefore, with this deep conviction that God is answering our prayer, that he is carrying out his commitment, his covenant, we immediately thank and praise him for the answer already received. This is a very practical way of bearing witness to, giving testimony to, our faith that God keeps his promise. We no sooner ask for something than we thank him and praise him for giving it. This is prophetic prayer in practice. It is our faith put into action; and, at the same time, it deepens our faith. When we pray alone in this way, we pray calmly and peacefully, for it drains the feverish anxiety out of us. When we share such a manner of praying with others, it is a witness to them of this commitment, this covenant of God, and a witness to our faith in his keeping his commitment. This helps us all to deepen our faith. It is very much the kind of prayer St. Paul meant when he wrote, in Philippians: "Dismiss all anxiety from your minds. Present your needs to God in every form of prayer and in petitions full of gratitude. Then God's own peace, which is beyond all understanding, will stand guard over your hearts and minds, in Christ Jesus" (4:6-7).

So covenant prayer is not only prophetic, it is a prayer of thanksgiving. We make thanksgiving and praise the beginning, the middle, and the conclusion of our prayer. In the light of this, we return to the thought of Our Lady with a clearer realization that she prayed in much the same way: that is the whole meaning of her Magnificat. It was a prophetic prayer. She began by praising God for his own greatness. She sang with joy that to her—she who was nothing—God was a mighty Savior. He had looked upon her, his servant, in her lowliness, and his regard had so blessed her that all the ages to come would call her blessed. God who is mighty, whose name is holy, had done great things for her. "It is done," she was saying, "it is done; he has done it for me." Not only to her but to all who fear him, all who obey him from age to age, he is merciful. She proclaims what he has done, what he is doing, what he will do.

God has thrust out his mighty arm and "confused the proud in their inmost thoughts." She was Queen of Liberation and Mother of the Oppressed as she sang: "He has deposed the mighty from their thrones and raised the lowly to high places. The hungry he has given every good thing, while the rich he has sent empty away." He kept the promise he made to her ancestors. "He has upheld Israel his servant, ever mindful of his mercy; even as he promised our fathers, promised Abraham and his descendants forever" (Lk 1:46-55).

Mary was proclaiming prophetically what God had done, the message that his power is mercy, and that he keeps his covenant. At the same time, she was foretelling that he would go on doing the same to his people forever. She was, for this reason, the Queen of Prophets and the leader of prophetic prayer. The "Hail Mary" of the Rosary continues this song of praise and thanksgiving that Mary began in her Magnificat. We ask her intercession for us "now." It is very much a biblical prayer, part of the covenant of her Son, and has no meaning apart from him.

St. Paul frequently urged his people to pray in the spirit of faith and continuous thanksgiving. To the people of Thessalonica he wrote, "Rejoice always, never cease praying, render constant thanks" (2 Thes 5:16-18). To the Ephesians: "Give thanks to God the Father always and for everything in the name of our Lord Jesus Christ" (Eph 5:20). Jesus is our covenant. God will infallibly fulfill his covenant in Jesus. He will keep his commitment. How natural and inevitable it is, then, that praying always should go beyond worship in church to praying alone or together in the home where the family spends so much of its time (Eph 5:18-19 and Col 3:16). We should pray at all times and pray with total confidence, and when possible, in response to God's word, alone or in a group.

Sharing God's word and responding with prayer is our preparation for the Eucharist, which is a renewal of the covenant and a great thanksgiving prayer for the covenant we have in Jesus and for what he has accomplished for us. Benediction service, being principally an adoration and praising of Jesus our Savior, is essentially a biblical blessing and praising of God.

As St. Paul says, we are to praise and thank God in all circumstances. That means, therefore, not just when things are going nicely. We should praise God and thank God also for what is difficult and painful. We should praise and thank God for loss and sorrow, for failure, for embarrassment. This is not in any sense a morbid delight in self-punishment to release guilt anxiety. Nor is it an escape mechanism, a praising in spite of a bad situation. Nor is it a way of bargaining with the Lord: "I'm praising you, therefore get me out of this." Rather, it is simply that we have complete confidence that God is there, still carrying out his commitment in these difficult circumstances, in these failures, in these defeats, in spite of all appearances to the contrary. He is still very much in control of his world, and he is present, drawing the best possible good out of everything that happens and that is, and even from what ought not to be.

So we thank God for the very situation, bad as it is, because it glorifies his wisdom, power, and mercy, "I willingly boast of my weakness instead, that the power of Christ may rest upon me" (2 Cor 12:9). "Everything is ordered to your benefit, so that the grace bestowed in abundance may bring greater glory to God because they who give thanks are many" (2 Cor 4:15). We look ahead in faith to see the good in the most difficult and impossible and seemingly contradictory things. Looking back, we can usually discern what God was about and see the good he chose mysteriously to achieve. The absolute power of God is always there, working out his wise purposes for our good.

This is the real and imperfect world in which we live among imperfect people like ourselves. It is the world that Jesus spoke about in the Beatitudes when he said, Blessed are they who are sorrowful, who suffer, who are badly treated, who are deprived. The Beatitudes took for granted that Christianity would not suddenly so change men that this world would become a paradise.

Yet Jesus meant what he said, "My peace is my gift to you; I do not give it to you as the world gives peace. Do not be distressed or fearful" (Jn 14:27). Jesus meant that harmony and union with God which was the seal of the covenant (Num 6:26-27). He meant us to have inner spiritual tranquility not only when everything looks fine and seems in order, but at all times; peace in the most difficult, the most painful circumstances, the most humiliating failures and defeats, because he is there, he our covenant and salvation. At every moment he is carrying out his covenant, accomplishing the best possible good for us. "Continually we carry about in our bodies the dying of Jesus, so that in our bodies the life of Jesus may also be revealed" (2 Cor 4:10). We can appreciate this spirit most fully if we consider Our Lord's words at the Last Supper. There, in spite of great heaviness of heart at the certainty of his passion and death, and very shortly before his agony in the garden, Jesus thanked and praised God as he made himself present in the new form of the Eucharist and said in the same breath that he was to be sacrificed for all men.

Permit me to repeat, can we doubt the power of prayer when

we remember that he has given us his power? "The man who has faith in me will do the works that I do" (Jn 14:12). He has given us his Holy Spirit. "The Paraclete, the Holy Spirit whom the Father will send in my name, will instruct you in everything" (Jn 14:26). He has given us his friendship. "I call you friends, since I have made known to you all that I heard from my Father" (Jn 15:15). He has given us his joy. "All this I tell you that my joy may be yours and your joy may be complete" (Jn 15:12). He wants us to fulfill our commitment, to accomplish what he asks of us, including "Ask. Seek. Knock." For his part, he wants to answer our prayers so that our joy will be complete.

How he is fulfilling his part of the covenant and why we should pray with great confidence through him is spelled out in the many riches of our inheritance that we find in chapter eight of Romans. One of those mercies is that since God has given his only Son, will he not also give every other blessing? "Is it possible that he who did not spare his own Son but handed him over for the sake of us all will not grant us all things besides?" (Rom 8:32).

So our praise and our thanksgiving simply express our faith in this commitment of God, this covenant that Jesus is, and also continually express the total surrender, the total trust, which God is waiting for and which, on our part, makes our prayers so powerful. Therefore, since we place everything in God's hands, trust God totally, then, through this thanksgiving and praise, we release into every circumstance the power of God.

This confidence in Jesus our covenant is the meaning of the boldness in the prayers of the liturgy. They take for granted that the most astounding things will be given us through Christ Our Lord. For how many years or even centuries have we prayed bold words with faint hearts? Have we taken seriously the prayers for bodily healings? Do we trust God to keep his word? Do we have the faith to fulfill his conditions and pray as he wants us to pray?

In any case, we praise, thank and trust, not necessarily because we feel like it (for we may feel just the opposite) but in obedience, because he wants us to. At times it may require us to go against our feelings —feelings of rebellion, sorrow, discouragement, depression. We have to grit our teeth at times, make the surrender, and go on praising and thanking him with the concentration of our full being.

There is something more. Starting with the fact that, as we have continually stressed, in God there is no time—no past, no present nor future—we can take for granted that since we have now come to this capacity of continually praising and thanking God in all circumstances, no matter what, God knows this prayer in the timelessness of his eternal mind. Therefore he can use it, and is using it, to make up for even our past mistakes and past failures. We are carrying forward everything from the past and placing it in the hands of God, with thanksgiving and praise. He draws out and goes on drawing out, even from the past, everything that is best for our welfare and the glory of God. Therefore we take for granted, too, that nothing has ever been an accident, that God had it in mind all the time, for he was there, in every circumstance, working out our human growth and spiritual salvation, making us more and more a part of his covenant and bringing us forward to a fuller faith, a fuller experience of this covenant that he has made with us.

Finally, by witnessing to all God's blessings and all that Jesus won for us by his death, resurrection, and ascension, we are continually, by thanksgiving and praise, joining Jesus in his warfare against the prince of darkness. We do not want to pervert time and our God-given gifts by witnessing to evil through our criticism, complaints, rebellion, and despair. That is doing the devil's work. We are on Christ's side, carrying forward his victory by hearts that sing with faith, hope, thanksgiving, and joy.

CHAPTER 13

Fellowship and Joy in Prayer

A Bible-prayer meeting is a gathering of Christians to hear God speak through his scriptural word and to answer by their prayers and sacred songs of praise and thanskgiving. God wants his people to praise and thank him as the source and center of everything.

The primary purpose of the meeting, therefore, is to worship God and thank him for his manifold blessings in the most sincere and spontaneous way; adoration and gratitude occupy the greater part of the time. Its secondary purpose, which comes as a consequence of the primary, is the inner transformation of the hearts and the lives of the participants and the formation, strengthening, and building up of a Christian community. It is from the linking up of such Christian communities that the total Christian community attains growth and solidarity, embodying and carrying forward the victory of Christ's redemption. Anyone who has had the happy experience of consistent participation in such shared prayer has been made aware of the change in his life; and, correspondingly, he has been conscious of his sense of deprivation when it has not been possible to participate regularly. For the effect has been spiritually debilitating: faith has seemed to slacken and prayer to become more difficult; God's presence has seemed less real and his word less alive; and the burdens of apostolic work have seemed to become heavier.

Perhaps it will help to clarify what shared prayer is by saying what it is not. For one thing, it is not shared meditation, even though this also serves its own good purpose by an interchange of ideas that come from reflecting together upon a Scripture passage or a relevant reading from other sources. Shared prayer is not a substitute for personal private prayer but rather supports and stimulates further private prayer. Another thing it is not is a discussion, though if a theme develops, a brief exchange on it can be helpful. (Some groups meet another night of the week for Bible study or discussion of pertinent topics.) Shared prayer is not teaching, even though quite commonly, and some insist essentially, there is some instruction by the leader or other indicated person on a point of Scripture or of Christian living. Anyone may ask for an explanation of a scriptural word or passage. All such instruction is accepted with an open heart and without entering into controversy.

Since one of its purposes is to form a Christian community, it is necessary that the group be localized so that it can grow naturally and spiritually together. While it may not grow out of a community—since they rarely exist, whether on natural, religious, or cultural grounds—the group, if localized, can at least grow into a human and Christian community by praying together, getting to know one another, establishing deep affective bonds of mutual concern, and working together to serve their fellow men either individually or in community matters. Only at the local level is it possible to have a relatively stable group who will meet regularly.

The kind of meeting depends on the kind of people who participate. This has nothing to do with status or age. There is no generation gap, no social or other kind of barrier. Education or lack of it, employment or profession, do not enter in. All are welcome and all participate, either silently or vocally, but always listening with an open heart and responding with prayer. "Each of us is a son of God because of your faith in Christ Jesus. All of you who have been baptized into Christ have clothed yourself with him. There does not exist among you Jew or Greek, slave or free man, male or female. All are one in Christ Jesus" (Gal 3:26-28). All who come to the Father in Jesus' name are children of God.

There is one kind of meeting that serves those who claim not to believe in God, or in Christ as God, and those who claim to believe but do not practice their belief and need to find Christ again. In such groups the number is preferably limited for the sake of dealing with individual needs. One of the believers guiding the "talk-it-over" session can begin with a prayer of Christ's presence and add thanksgiving and praise. Then each of the group could be asked his or her name, place of residence, occupation, etc. If they care to volunteer any details of their religious background, they may do so. Then comes the key question that must be handled with respect and delicacy: "Would you care to tell us what attracted you to come?" This often leads to an exchange in greater depth and may bring out some problems that call for counseling and encouragement. Sooner or later it is in place to read some passages from the New Testament on God's mercy, the need of faith, and the new man each one is in Christ. Also helpful are the testimonies of two or three who have moved from confusion to peace through their encounter with Christ as Savior. Jesus loves all and wants all to come to him.

There is another kind of meeting for believers who come seeking a new experience of God but are unaccustomed to praying out loud directly to God in a group. They need an explanation of a Christ-centered life and how it relates people to one another in prayer, love, and mutual service—all in response to God's living word. The place of the Holy Spirit in Christian life also needs explanation. The need of experiencing mutual support and joy in a Christian community is not always clear to many people, even though unconsciously desired. It is helpful if some of the leaders give a little history of Bible-prayer meetings and their basis in Scripture, as well as some of their fruits. Then, after a little break, a regular Bible-prayer meeting could begin. What matters is that all pray to the Father in Jesus' name and learn to know his love.

Then there are meetings of those already initiated, who already know one another and are accustomed to participating personally. With a minimum of leadership and great openness to the Spirit, they move easily through a rhythm of Bible reading, prayer, singing, and back again, for two or three hours. They meet regularly at least once a week. They come because they experience a human warmth and friendliness in the group and a spiritual support and growth through uniting themselves to God and one another in a Christian community at prayer. The size of such groups may vary from ten persons to five hundred. The leaders, and some others who have had long experience with such gatherings and feel the need to grow still more in the Spirit, make it a point to meet separately in small groups in addition to the large group meetings, either for prayer or for study.

In any case, people are coming to Jesus in their own way, the way he lays out for them. He loves them and wants them to understand his love. This they can do only by following the way he has chosen for them, by putting away fears and anxieties, by relaxing in his love and listening to his word. Before him we are all children, and we must learn to trim ourselves down to size and learn a childlike trust in Jesus, with a child's eagerness to love, praise, and thank him. His true children are those who have learned to know his love, who do his work and show his love in the way he pointed out to them.

As for the setting of the meetings, there should be a minimum of noise and physical distraction. Preferably, the participants should sit facing each other, and everyone should speak loud enough to be heard by everyone else. Some discourage the presence of young children, lest they create a disturbance at crucial points of prayer. Others find little difficulty in this because the children seem to sense that something very sacred and important, even mysterious, is going on and want to be part of it. Hence they are on their best behavior. Besides, they seem happy to be allowed to participate in something with their fathers and mothers and other grownups. Clearly, Jesus wants children at the meetings, but they must learn to be quiet.

The most important preparation is the personal life of each participant, especially his prayer-life. If the community prayer is to grow, it has to be through the personal growth of the members. The quality of the individual's prayer is what surfaces in the group. Personal prayer should be nourished by daily reading of the Bible, with reflection on God's word. It requires, above all, the self-forgetfulness needed to serve others with affection and joy, especially those closest to us. It depends, also, on the courage to witness to what God is doing and saying among us, i.e., whenever prudent opportunity permits. Some people will never know of his love until someone tells them.

As we have continually stressed, it is important that we continue to pray whether we feel like it or not, even to the point of thanking and praising God for what seems most difficult, most worrisome and contradictory, for God is there also, drawing the best possible good out of everything for us. God does not change because of the changing circumstances of our lives. More specifically, members should pray for the spiritual renewal of all men, for the fruit of the Bible-prayer meetings, for all who come to participate, and for the leaders.

Members should think out ahead of time what they are going to share, out of love, with their brothers and sisters in Christ: a passage of Scripture; a blessing of God in their own lives or the lives of relatives or friends, or in the local community, the nation, or the world. Everyone should come with an open heart, ready to receive whatever God may wish to say to him or do in and through him. This preparation in no way hinders the spontaneity of the meeting itself. But if meetings go dead, very often it is because there has not been the necessary spiritual preparation and growth in the members. The loss of vitality and spiritual profit may also be due to too little praise and thanskgiving, too much discussion, faulty leadership, or individuals who monopolize the attention of others or become argumentative.

The less structure there is in a Bible-prayer meeting the better. Shared prayer should be spontaneous, freely and openly sensitive to what the Spirit seems to suggest. This does not exclude the careful preparation of the leader, for he must be ready to supply whatever is needed to encourage participation and keep the meeting moving. But the less the leader has to say the better, for that means each participant is sensitive to the Holy Spirit and is responding in a way that benefits all.

Spontaneity does not exclude a loose outline, or general direction, that a meeting may follow. For example, it is fairly common that a meeting starts with a leader recalling in direct prayer the presence of Jesus. Then follows thanksgiving, praise, witnessing, testimony, for all that God has done and is doing. There should also be the expression of the responsibility of love towards ourselves and towards others in petitions. This outline should not be rigid but fluid: the elements are spontaneously interchangeable. Some prefer to start with a song, followed by recollection and silence. Then a psalm is read slowly and clearly, followed by silence and prayer. Or shared prayer may be completely unstructured, though still biblical.

Shared prayer is strongly biblical. Everyone should have a Bible, or at least a New Testament. Anyone at any time may express the desire to share a certain scriptural passage either by reading it himself or asking that someone else read it. If, as the meeting goes on, a theme develops, the readings should preferably be related to the theme. Each waits until the others have found the place before reading, for this is a sharing of God's word. God speaks to us through his word. We cannot be silent. Our response is prayer and song.

Anyone at any time may suggest a religious song. "Who sings well prays twice." The songs may be cheerful, celebrating the redemption or God's glory and goodness, but they are always sung prayer. They may also be deeply meditative. Guitar accompaniment adds to the cheerfulness and enjoyment. It is not a song fest, but we are an Easter people, a resurrection people, on the way to eternal happiness, and we should act like it. "You are a chosen race, a royal priesthood, a holy nation, a people he claims for his own to proclaim the glorious works of the One who called you from darkness into his marvelous light" (1 Pt 2:9). Music is a gift of God's love. He likes to hear his people rejoicing in his love by singing praise to the Father.

As for petitions, a person may express his own petition or ask another to pray for this need. Some feel that it is always preferable that another pray for a particular person's need, rather than the person himself, for in this way there is a sharing of mutual concern. The members simply express their affirmation of the petition by an added phrase or sentence. But there should be a time for everyone to ask the Father in Jesus' name for their needs. They should look to Jesus for everything. He will hear all prayers made to the Father in his name.

Petitions are made in strong awareness that Jesus is our covenant and that he has committed the Father to grant anything we ask in his name. Hence each petition concludes always with thanking and praising Jesus for the answer already given. As we have repeatedly stressed, in God there is no time; he sees both the prayer and its answer in the one eternal now. And he can do anything. Covenanted prayer is prophetic prayer (Mt 18:19-20). For the same reasons, along with the petitions, we thank and praise God for what seems like impossible, difficult, and contradictory situations; God is always there and always in control of his world.

The content of Bible-prayer meetings excludes public confessions and complaints, though one may pray briefly for forgiveness. The meetings are totally positive, a thanking God for all the good he has done and is doing. Each is a step of the redemption carried forward. Each witnesses to the victory of Christ—criticism and complaints are a witnessing to evil and to the work of the devil who makes war against Christ. Moreover, shared prayer should not be used to plead for the correction of one's neighbor's faults. True prayer is based on humble awareness of personal faults and filled with love for others. Besides, any suggestion of the negative tends to awaken negative, defensive feelings that hinder one's response to the Holy Spirit and make a person close up.

Since the man's role in everything, including religion, is normally to be active, it is generally desirable that the leadership be dominantly male. This will encourage the presence of men as well as their participation. Men often do not care to speak up, much less pray, in the presence of women. But they must keep an active role, for otherwise women will dominate the meetings and men will drop out entirely. To avoid this possibility, some groups of beginners have accepted a practice of always having a man initiate the spontaneous prayer, even though it means waiting in silence until a man speaks, and thereafter alternate men and women until the principle is well established. Normally, women welcome the leadership of men, especially in spiritual matters. Since God made man the natural head of the family, it follows that he wants to work through the man also as the spiritual head. In any case, when a team provides the leadership, women can be part of the team. Nevertheless there are times when only women can lead the meeting because they have known Jesus' love longer than the men present. Women are then to lead until the men have grown in their love of Jesus. Men will listen to a woman when she is doing God's work and showing his love.

Participation, whether of men or women, includes vocal prayer, suggestions about scripture passages and about songs, giving testimony to the goodness of God, witnessing to his working in individual lives and in the world, petitions and prayer requests, manifesting the gifts of the Holy Spirit, etc.

Each participant comes to the meeting fully open to what God wishes to say through him or to him. Shared prayer is difficult at first for most people because they are not accustomed to pray out loud in the presence of others. Each should take for granted that what he feels prompted to say comes from the Holy Spirit and is meant not only for himself but also for someone else in the group. It nearly always happens that what one person says is a help to some other person. At times, instead of praying out loud, a person should pray to Jesus about what he feels is important for someone else in the meeting. All should pray silently to Jesus before praying out loud.

At the appropriate time, each member should break through his natural fears and timidity and pray out loud, directly to Jesus, to the Father, or to the Holy Spirit. It should not be an indirect prayer, in the third person, e.g., "I thank God that . . . ". This mastering of fears represents a human and Christian growth that puts people on top of blind emotions and makes them free and trustful. They can accept themselves better because they experience themselves being accepted for their true selves that come out in prayer. They trust and are trusted. Participants support one another in mutual growth.

Hence they must learn to relax in Jesus' love, and as they do they will know how much he loves them.

This trust is strongly dependent upon the affective warmth of the group. This affective warmth supplies a deep need because of the affective starvation in the depersonalized environment of urban, industrialized, and institutionalized life. But quite apart from its corrective value, which serves as one more "sign of the times," there is a normal need to express genuinely felt affection. This natural and normal expression of affection is also the important natural basis of the formation of a true Christian community among the members. It is one more way in which we see the sound psychology of the New Testament. Jesus rebuked the Pharisee for not greeting him with a kiss (Lk 7:45). Both St. Paul and St. Peter encourage a Christian warmth among their people by directing them to greet one another with a "holy kiss" or a "holy embrace" (Rom 12:16, 1 Cor 16:20, 2 Cor 13:12, 2 Thes 5:26, 1 Pt 5:14). Initial greetings are brief. Instead of continued conversation, it is better for each one to settle down in recollection and reading and reflection on the Scriptures.

During the meeting, each should pay full attention to God and not to self or to others. The God-centeredness of the prayer is essential to its depth. This achieves at once a self-purification and a sensitiveness to the Spirit.

At the same time, through sharing God's word, through prayer, song, and thanksgiving, and through the working of the Holy Spirit, there is experienced a growing sense of fellowship in the Holy Spirit. There is a deep personal concern in everyone for every other person present. This extends to personal sharing and counseling after the meeting, over a cup of coffee, and to positive help on other occasions. This love for one's brother or sister in Christ shows the love of Jesus for them. The group is in no sense ingrown but rather outgoing, apostolic, and service-orientated in the Christian community. We make the love of Jesus visible for all men by doing his work, loving our neighbor, and going to the Father in his name. We should pray especially to be the instruments of his love.

When a group is composed of people who have a habit of prayer, extended moments of shared silence are frequent. Usually, the more mature in prayer a group is, the richer are the silences, since all are sharing intensely the presence of God. Hence no one is ever embarrassed by silence, for it is always filled with prayer. There are many ways to pray, and no one should be afraid to be silent in Jesus' love.

Often a theme develops as the prayer moves spontaneously along. Both leaders and the members should be sensitive to this and follow the theme through as much as possible, because through concentrating on one theme the group allows the Holy Spirit to deepen the faith and confidence of all present. There should, however, be no rigidity about this. The Holy Spirit may choose to work through different themes and needs. The important thing is that we pray together in Christ.

Bible-prayer meetings are the usual preparation, though not the only one, for receiving the baptism of the Holy Spirit we have already spoken of. This baptism should be prepared for, prayed for, and sought. Through this inflow of the Spirit's presence and power, the person normally experiences great inner peace, coordination, confidence, joy, and warm affection and kindliness towards everyone. The Scriptures come alive with the presence of Jesus. A person experiences what it means to be a "new creature," a "new man" in Christ in the fellowship of the Holy Spirit. And the gifts of the Spirit become active. As all come to the Father in Jesus' name, so all should receive the baptism of the Holy Spirit when they are old enough to ask the Father for it. The Father will give each one the gifts he needs to do God's work and show his love. God wants all men to love the Father, Son, and Holy Spirit and to learn to love as men are made to love.

For the exercise of their apostolate,

> the Holy Spirit who sanctifies the People of God through the ministry and the sacraments gives to the faithful special gifts as well (cf. 1 Cor 12:7), "allotting to everyone according as he will" (1 Cor 12:11). Thus may the individuals, "according to the gift that each has received, administer it to one another" and become "good stewards of the manifold grace of God" (1 Pt 4:10), and build up thereby the whole body in charity (cf. Eph 4:16). From the reception of these charisms or gifts, including those which are

less dramatic, there arise for each believer the right and duty to use them in the Church and in the world for the good of mankind and for the upbuilding of the Church. In so doing, the believers need to enjoy the freedom of the Holy Spirit who "breathes where he wills" (Jn 3:8). At the same time, they must act in communion with their brothers in Christ, especially with their pastors. The latter must make a judgment about the true nature and proper use of these gifts, not in order to extinguish the Spirit, but to test all things and hold fast to what is good (cf. 1 Thes. 5:12, 19, 21). (Vatican II, Decree on the Apostolate of the Laity, no. 3)

The Committee on Doctrine of the American Bishops reported (Nov. 14, 1969) in a similar vein about the charismatic gifts. They said that the right approach is "not the denial of their existence but their proper use." This is outlined by St. Paul:

When you assemble, one has a psalm, another some instruction to give, still another a revelation to share; one speaks in tongues, another interprets. All well and good, so long as everything is done with a constructive purpose. If any are going to talk in tongues, let it be at most two or three, each in turn, with another to interpret what they are saying. But if there is no one to interpret, there should be silence in the assembly, each one speaking only to himself and to God. Let no more than two or three prophets speak, and let the rest judge the worth of what they say. If another, sitting by, should happen to receive a revelation, the first one should then keep quiet. You can all speak your prophecies, but one by one, so that all may be instructed and encouraged. The spirits of the prophets are under the prophets' control, since God is a God, not of confusion, but of peace. (1 Cor 14:26-33)

This shows the indispensable need to listen to God's word and prompting, to relax in his love and look to him for everything, so as to understand Jesus' work and show his love.

In regard to the fruits of Bible-prayer groups, the Bishops' Committee advised the prudence of observing

the effects on those who participate in the prayer meetings. There are many indications that this participation leads to a better understanding of the role the Christian plays in the Church. Many have experienced progress in their spiritual life. They are attracted to the reading of the Scriptures and a deeper understanding of their faith. They seem to grow in their attachment to certain established devotional patterns such as devotion to the Real Presence and the Rosary. (Ibid.)

Most important of all, since Jesus shows his love for men through men, they will know his love and know it is given to all men when they share his word together with a relaxed listening.

These fruits of Bible-prayer meetings can be elaborated somewhat. A major concern about them must be pastoral because great numbers of people of every age and social level, but especially among the young, have withdrawn from the regular practice of institutionalized religion. This applies to every denomination. Now through Bible-prayer meetings they are finding God again. And since there is no generation or any other kind of gap in the meetings, they have great Christian and pastoral value. If only in charity (which is a rather large "if!"), they become the responsibility of every part of the Christian community. They are also, as experience demonstrates, an excellent way to form authentic Christian communities. Moreover, Roman Catholics discover or rediscover a dimension of God's love that is difficult to experience elsewhere.

Shared prayer in these meetings very commonly leads to a transformation of one's personal prayer, and for a good reason. Once a person becomes accustomed to saying out loud in the presence of others exactly what he means and only what he means and, very importantly, at the rhythm at which he can experience meaning it, he never again wants to pray out loud a single word that does not come from the depths of his being. This makes for deep sincerity as well as for leisurely, meditative praise and petition. Besides, shared prayer noticeably encourages continual prayer.

As we have already said, shared prayer also serves certain natural needs apart from increased sincerity. It is a means to human growth. By saying out loud what is deep within his true self, a person finds that he can speak out and has, therefore, conquered fears and is more of a free human being in command of himself. Equally important is the fact that he finds himself accepted just as he is, with his thoughts, and thus is paying a debt to his Creator. He is serving others by confirming, supporting, encouraging them. He is experiencing the concern of others for himself and gladly reciprocates with concern for them. He experiences community and fellowship, plus the friendship of the Holy Spirit. He experiences and gives trust and affective warmth. Hence the restful sense of peace, well-being, and joy that fills a person at the end of a meeting.

At the supernatural level, the two or more hours of shared prayer are a repeated exercise of faith in God's living word and an ever deepening experience of faith. The blessings for which members thank God, the many testimonies to God's presence, power, and love confirm and deepen one's faith in God's fidelity to his word and in his presence, power, and goodness. Within this atmosphere of freedom, uncritical acceptance, faith, and love, the spiritual gifts grow and develop as a normal part of the Bible-prayer meeting from the beginning. Some recommend that if gifts like prophecy, tongues, and interpretation do not immediately emerge, they should nevertheless from the beginning be prayed for explicitly, and joyously accepted when they do occur. This will not seem strange to a God-centered, Spirit-filled community at worship, for such gifts are signs among believers (Mk 16:17).

What matters above all is the worship of God that many experience as a necessary supplement to formal Sunday worship. Scarcely less in value is the mutual love and affection that shows the presence and action of the Holy Spirit. Then there is the joy that does not exclude a healthy seriousness and is its own sign of God's presence. There is an absence of anxiety, for they cast all their cares upon him who cares for all (1 Pt 5:7). Hence the peace and peacefulness, a resting in God. All men who come to the Father in Jesus' name and learn to relax in his love will experience his love profoundly.

Finally, a few brief notes about starting a group. In general, we may say that God takes a strong initiative and seems to require a minimum of human effort. If he wants a Bible-prayer group, he seems to open the way through someone inquiring about such a thing. It is not wise to try to pressure anyone into coming. Mention it only once to those who seem open to the idea and then wait for them to ask. Neither is it wise to phone people before each meeting to ask if they are coming. Since Jesus said (Mt 18:19), "If two or three are agreed," it could well be that two or three might find themselves praying alone for months and months before God sends others to join. God may want the two or three to become "firmly grounded and steadfast" (Col 1:23) until "charity be the root and foundation" (Eph 3:17) of their lives. It pays to spend time on the quality of the foundation of any structure. The nucleus of the group then are prepared to be good leaders. The increase in numbers will come when God finds them ready. It is not recommended that a person go to a meeting just to find out what it is like, for no two meetings are alike; and there are no spectators —only participants who come to pray and worship God. There should be a definite commitment to go to a minimum of five meetings. And it is valuable at times to go to different kinds of meetings in order to sense the range of possibilities. The important thing is that God wants all men to come to him because he loves them. He wants them to know the peaceful warmth of his tender care so that they can lead others to the same experience.

By these informal prayer meetings that spring from God's word and burst into happy song, we are simply rediscovering and obeying what God directed us to do from the very beginning:

> Be filled with the Spirit, addressing one another in psalms and hymns and inspired songs. Sing praise to the Lord with all your hearts. Give thanks to God the Father always and for everything in the name of our Lord Jesus Christ. Defer to one another out of reverence for Christ . . . . Let the word of Christ, rich as it is, dwell in you. In wisdom made perfect, instruct and admonish one another. Sing gratefully to God from your hearts in psalms, hymns, and inspired songs. (Eph 5:18-21; Col 3:16-17)

St. Paul was speaking in these passages of prayer meetings in homes. In First Corinthians he seems to refer also to more official gatherings (1 Cor 14:26-28).

Through meeting thus in love and hearing God's word in an atmosphere of continual sincere prayer, "you will be able to grasp fully, with all the holy ones, the breadth and length and height and depth of Christ's love, and experience this love which surpasses all knowledge, so that you may attain to the fullness of God himself" (Eph 3:18-19).

CHAPTER 14

Towards Contemplative Prayer

Christianity is centered at once in being and becoming, in living with the life of Christ and becoming like him, but never in a labyrinth of abstractions, whether philosophical, theological, or moralistic. Analytical study is indispensable to the progress of thought, but what matters is that it should serve our human development, not enthrone itself and demand our worship. This is not to be in any sense anti-intellectual, but only to say that all theology produces its greatest fruit when it ends in the silence of contemplation.

Contemplation is the experience of God, not as an object of knowledge in an "I-Thou" relationship but in self-forgetfullness as simply "all"—all that there is. As we have observed earlier in this book, our age is passionately in quest of truth, being, reality—all to be sincerely lived and shared in mutual responsibility to one another. We are orientated to community in our thinking, and more and more in our living.

Perhaps precisely because rapid cultural change often destroys entrenched concepts of God, contemplation has flourished in times of crisis. While the Roman Empire was crumbling, the life of the spirit flourished; saints clustered round about the great Augustine, whose *Confessions* became the spiritual manual for all of Christendom until another cultural change produced the *Imitation of Christ*. In the religiously and culturally disturbed century which preceded the posting of Luther's theses on the church doors at Wittenburg there was a saint born every year. In our times, so full of shock and strain, we see a resurgence of the desire for prayer and contemplation in every sector of society, our young adults included. Bible distribution has reached an almost incredible extension, and the classics of mysticism are greatly in demand.

This development is what we should expect: it is the fruit of the theological and spiritual vitality which first showed itself in mid-nineteenth century along with the beginning of the democratic age in the social revolutions that rocked Europe at the same time. Now, given that this spiritual renewal comes to us alongside a materialism which seems to threaten the very existence of religious faith, some may ask how genuine and durable it can be supposed to be. But what matters is that God has shown his presence so strongly, silencing all the talk we were hearing such a short time ago about God being dead. There is no point in waiting to see whether the renewed interest in the experience of God is going to burst like a bubble because it is so contrary to other factors in the environment. It is much more to the point to encourage and guide this renewal through our participation, while we leave it to God to decide whether it is to permeate all of society or only prepare a new "remnant in Israel" to survive some great storm of the future.

In any case, this much is clear: the movement towards community among men is the reflection on earth of the reality of the divine life. For the ultimate being we know, whose truth we speak in words, is a community being—a community of three persons who are the one God. He is the one being who forever is, without dependence upon anyone or upon time, without change or need to be perfected. He is the one being who alone can say, "I am who am" (Ex 3:14).

We cannot imitate God and say, "I am who am." At most, we must always say, "By God's favor I am what I am" (1 Cor 15:10). And what I am is not absolute, unchanging being but always becoming, always changing. Yet in us change is not like shifting sand in the desert that blows in the wind; indeed, unlike all the other living things around us, we do not experience the final change which is dissolution, for we have a permanent hold on our spiritual reality. We come into being through God's creative act to become each one a unique, unmatched human person who spends a brief flash between eternities in the becoming that is our one life on earth. It is our destiny to go on to live eternally with God in a new, glorious, and final state of resurrection in which we shall see him forever face to face.

In the meantime, taking ourselves existentially, we find ourselves a strange mixture of something and nothing: utterly ·unworthy of anything and yet, by divine condescension, counted worthy of a thousand daily gifts, including God's gift of himself shared with men in countless ways. We must be perpetually grateful, because everything we are comes from the Creator and we are committed by our very nature to return his gifts. Even in our giving back we are at the same time receiving, for he gives being and reality to our action of thanksgiving, gives us the impulse to gratitude and to express it in community as witnesses to one another. Through this return of all things to God, we in our creaturely littleness enter into the divine immensity by completing the eternal circle of life that begins, centers, and ends in God. This wise humility is an indispensable step to contemplation.

But now, having seen our own nothingness without God, how shall we enter into the mystery that is God? One of the ways (but it should not be given more attention than it deserves, for it is only one way) is to remove from our concept of God every sort of lack or limitation. We are all made to approach him partly by this way of denial (apophatic theology)—that is, by sweeping away all that is not God. We try to know the Creator and Supreme Being by removing from his pure being every imperfection we can think of. Later we will return to some necessary distinctions on this point. But for the moment we may say in general that the Indian Upanishads and the practitioners of Zen who followed the northern Chinese school of Shen Hsiu call it the stripping away of all images and ideas. The Hindu contemplative seeks to become Godlike by saying, "Not this, not this!" to every thought, image, or feeling that comes to his consciousness. The Taoist of China says: "The names that can be named are not the changeless Name"—which is not wholly unrelated to St. John of the Cross's repeatedly saying, "It is all nothing, nothing." And St. Teresa of Avila said, "All things pass. God's love alone remains." Yes, every created being, truth, beauty, joy, knowledge, or power has its limits and imperfections. These created things cannot be God. At best they tell us more of what God is not than of what he is.

But at least we do experience these imperfect things. And since they do exist, they have a cause, and that cause we call God. So we go to God also by way of cause. But how far can we go? In God there is perfect unity of being; he is absolutely and totally one; nothing in him is fragmented, dissipated nor beyond complete control. And in God all things are one; essence and existence are one, both equally unknown in the fullness they have in God. Even the best of valid proofs show only that the great unknown we call God actually *is*, as the necessary source upon which everything depends. Without God as the great unknown, the unknown source of everything, there would be no minds to be mystified and no words to speak of mystery.

At best our words have no more range or value in speaking about God than does our knowledge of God. All our human words, including the word God, took their meaning originally from created things and are at best only reflections of the boundless being and inacessible light in which God dwells, the cloud of unknowing. Our human words do not tell us much about God. They can only be applied to God like—to use a fantastic analogy—baby clothes on a giant. Used with reference to God, they are immeasurably expanded and take on a depth of meaning that is beyond our grasp. All we can say is that their new meaning has some relationship to things with which we are familiar. That is about all we can know. That is why theology must ultimately end in the silence of contemplation if it is to achieve its final purpose and not become an obstacle by becoming an end in itself.

It is great wisdom to know that we do not understand too much about God. We know only that such things in us as being, reality, thought, love, have some resemblance to such things in God. God is uniquely different. He is almost totally other.

He alone could say, "I am who am. I must be." We do not have to be. God does. God is for real; he is love; he is being that is absolute and free. He owes us nothing beyond what he freely commits himself to give. He is complete master of himself and of the universe. He is the Lord of time and of history. He is inexpressible, unutterable, transcendent.

To return briefly to Zen and St. John of the Cross, let me quote Thomas Merton:

> Like all forms of Buddhism, Zen seeks an "Enlightenment" which results from the resolution of all subject-object relationships and oppositions in a pure void. But to call this void a mere negation is to reestablish the oppositions which are resolved in it. This explains the peculiar insistence of the Zen masters on "neither affirming nor denying." Hence it is impossible to attain "satori" (enlightenment) merely by quietistic inaction or the suppression of thought. Yet at the same time "enlightenment" is not an experience or activity of a thinking and self-conscious subject. Still less is it a vision of Buddha, or an experience of an "I-Thou" relationship with a Supreme Being considered as object of knowledge and perception. However, Zen does not *deny* the existence of a Supreme Being either. It neither affirms nor denies, it simply *is*. One might say that Zen is the ontological grasp of being in its "suchness" and "thusness" . . . The Zen insight is a direct grasp of being in itself, but not an intuition of the nature of being.[1]

Merton praises the Zen of Hui Neng (southern school of China), who revolutionized Buddhist spirituality

> by discounting the practice of formal and prolonged meditation, referred to as "zazen" ("sitting in meditation"). He placed no confidence in self-emptying introversion . . . For Hui Neng, *all life was Zen*. Zen could not be found merely by turning away from active life to become absorbed in meditation. Zen is the very awareness of the dynamism of life living itself in us—and awareness of itself, in us, as being the one life that lives in all . . . . The great merit of Hui Neng's Zen is that it liberates the mind from servitude to imagined spiritual states as "objects" which too easily become hypostatized and turn into idols that obsess and delude the seeker. In this, the Zen of Hui Neng comes rather close to the Gospels and St. Paul, though on an ontological rather than on a specifically religious level.[2]

Referring to Zen as unattainable by "mirror-wiping" meditation and possible only by "self-forgetfulness in the existential
present of life here and now," Merton says:

> This reminds us of St. John of the Cross and his teaching that
> the "Spiritual Way" is falsely conceived if it is thought to be a
> denial of flesh, sense, and vision in order to arrive at higher spiritual
> experience. On the contrary, the "dark night of sense" which sets
> the house of flesh at rest is at best a serious beginning. The true
> dark night is that of the spirit, where the "subject" of all higher
> forms of vision and intelligence is itself darkened and left in empti-
> ness: not as a mirror, pure of all impressions, but as a void without
> knowledge and without any natural capacity to know the super-
> natural. It is an error to think that St. John of the Cross teaches
> denial of the body and the senses as a way to reach a higher
> and more secret mystical knowledge. On the contrary, he teaches
> that the light of God shines in all emptiness where there is no
> natural subject to receive it. To this emptiness there is in reality
> no definite way. "To enter upon the way is to leave the way,"
> for the way itself is emptiness.[3]

> True emptiness is that which transcends all things, and yet is
> immanent in all. For what seems to be pure emptiness in this
> case is pure being. The character of emptiness, at least for the
> Christian contemplative, is pure love, pure freedom. Love that
> is free of everything, not determined by anything, or held down
> by any special relationship. It is love for love's sake. It is a sharing,
> through the Holy Spirit, in the infinite charity of God.[4]

Therefore, while we rightly study dogmatic and mystical
theology in order to know all we can and thus guide our thinking
and feed our prayer, at times our free will must tell the mind
to stop its restless activity, until with our whole being we can
say, "Be silent before our God." And however openly alert we
must be to all the reality, truth, and beauty of God taught us
by persons and things, at times we must say to all the world,
"Be dumb. Be silent. You can tell us that God is but you cannot
tell us what he is." "God is hidden, the God of Israel, the
savior" (Is 45:15).

If we are to approach the God who hides himself, we must
free ourselves from the attachment of mind and will to the things

of the world which are less than God. If we become satisfied with our knowledge or image of God, we are in danger of idolatry: the corruption of the best becomes the worst. Ideas are only representations: they are not God himself.

Virtues are not God, and our preoccupation with cataloguing and scoring up virtues can keep us from him. Spiritual bookkeeping is not prayer. Our concentration should be on God himself and on his love for us. The quest for self-fulfillment is not the quest for God, though only in seeking him shall we fulfill ourselves. Saints seek self-fulfillment as Christ sought it, through obedience to the divine will. Christ is the way, the truth, and the life.

On the Feast of St. Nicolas, St. Thomas Aquinas was taken beyond words and images in a great mystical experience. Thereafter, during the three months before his death, he deliberately refrained from writing another word of the *Summa Theologica*. He said that all he had written was just so much straw.

In the story of Job, God shows us how all human images and illusions may be tested and destroyed in mental and physical suffering; and on the cross Our Lord shows us the extremity of anguish possible to his perfect human nature in the mysterious experience of abandonment in which he cried out, echoing the cry of the suffering servant of Psalm 22: "My God, my God, why have you forsaken me?" (Mk 15:34).

St. John says: "No one has ever seen God" (Jn 1:18). Even in heaven we shall not have a perfect idea of God, for ideas are only representations, images seen cloudily in the mirror of the mind. In heaven we shall know him directly, face to face (1 Cor 13:12).

Through our abandonment to faith we are following St. John of the Cross, who teaches that the soul

> must not only be in darkness with respect to that part that concerns the creatures and temporal things . . . but likewise it must be blinded and darkened according to the part which has respect to God and spiritual things, which is the rational and higher part . . . . It must be like to a blind man leaning upon dark faith, taking it for guide and light, and leaning upon none of the things that he understands, experiences, feels and imagines. And if he

is not blinded as to this, and remains not in total darkness, he
attains not to that which is greater—namely, that which is taught
by faith.[5]

So we take the guidance of St. John Chrysostom: Let us invoke
him as the inexpressible God, incomprehensible, invisible and
unknowable; let us avow that he surpasses all power of human
speech, that he eludes the grasp of every mortal intelligence,
that the angels cannot penetrate him nor the seraphim see him
clearly, nor the cherubim fully understand him, for he is invisible
to the principalities and powers, the virtues and all creatures
without exception; only the Son and the Holy Spirit know him.[6]

To keep in proper balance the movement from the visible
and known to the invisible and incomprehensible, we must know
that all that has been said and written about "dark contemplation" and the "night of the senses" must

> not be misinterpreted to mean that the normal culture of the senses,
> of artistic taste, of imagination, and of intelligence should be for-
> mally renounced by anyone interested in a life of meditation and
> prayer. On the contrary, such culture is presupposed. One cannot
> go beyond what one has not yet attained, and normally the realiza-
> tion that God is "beyond images, symbols and ideas" dawns only
> on one who has previously made a good use of these things
> . . . . The function of image, symbol, poetry, music, chant and
> of ritual (remotely related to sacred dance) is to open up the inner
> self of the contemplative, to incorporate the senses and the body
> in the totality of the self-orientation to God that is necessary for
> worship and for meditation.[7]

On the other hand, the person who is sincerely seeking God
enters a state in which external circumstances are indifferent
to him. After twelve years in a Chinese prison, Bishop James
E. Walsh said, "For a man who likes to pray, prison is paradise."
What really matters is the readiness to humble ourselves, to
do ourselves the violence necessary to break out of our old shells
and respond actively to the new spiritual growth God is always
waiting to give us. Then with each new closeness to God, each
new light, we will feel more intensely that we never really knew
God before and be more ready to throw away what is "but

straw." We are made to walk towards God, the great Unknown, through ways that are as unknown to us at this moment as the saint's final experience of God is unknown to him on the day of his first conversion. "How deep are the riches and the wisdom and the knowledge of God! How inscrutable his judgments, how unsearchable his ways!" (Rom 11:33).

The world of mystery is our normal Christian atmosphere, as natural to us as the air we breathe. Therefore we cannot know the meaning of the world nor of ourselves nor of others nor of the community if we do not have the faith to look beyond the visible and tangible. When we live in Christ our whole day becomes a worship of mystery which embraces both God and the unfathomable depths of the human persons we are in community before God.

But the world of mystery that God is does not remain wholly outside of us. Through baptism God entered into each of us, sealed us with the Christ-mark as the one community which is his mystical Self and made us tabernacles of the divine life and divine persons. We bear the Infinite in our fragile hearts. Christ's promise, his mission, are already fulfilled in us in principle: "I came that they might have life and have it to the full" (Jn 10:10). But he will not take possession of us without our consent. Aware of our responsibility to one another, we must enter into the divine world within us in the silence of recollection, worship, and contemplation. If we ignore it, we are like beggars starving at a banquet table. If we treasure it as more precious than the whole universe about us, then indeed we have abundant life.

Sad to say, we come as worse than beggars; we come to God as sinners who have often been indicted for treason against his kingdom. We come enmeshed in a web of pride, fears, and misplaced love; full of the noise of those selfish preoccupations which shut out the whispering of God's grace in the soul. We come with too much of our hope centered in our own puny abilities and in the guidance of our natural impulses of the moment, without even knowing how helpless we are to do anything of ourselves in the supernatural world of our adoption.

This evil of our ignorance is its own mystery. And in the measure that we think and act as if we by our own powers could grasp God's world and manage it and keep it within certain bounds, to that extent we play the fool. We must come to God on our knees to receive the faith to enter into the mystery of our own person, the mystery of every other person, the mystery of the community person which is the mystical Person of Christ, and ultimately into the mystery of God.

Christ is the supreme dialogue between God and man. Through him and in him we encounter God, and ultimately it is through him that we enter into contemplative prayer. He spoke in terms we could understand—kingdom, vine and branches, friends, mother, father and son. He consecrated the world of nature to divine purposes by using visible and tangible things—water, oil, bread and wine, our human gestures—as channels of divine life in the seven sacraments he instituted. Centering in the sacrament of unity, the Eucharist, these sacraments continue in the present all the great works of the Old and New Testaments. Each is a personal encounter with Christ in which Christ comes to us and acts through us and upon us, and we come to him and let him heal and redeem us for our resurrection glory. And they stand in time for the fulfillment and completion of his work of restoring all things and giving them back to the Father in the eternal kingdom which is beyond time.

In the meantime of life we have work to do for God and for one another. Already made the children of God by adoption and living with the life of faith, we are not to seek our own ways in life but to grow serenely in his; not to seize by violence what we think will complete our happiness but trust in his divine providence. We must not be like Eve, who, in defiance of God's command, reached out for what she thought would free her from human limitations and make her wise. For the fruit of the tree of knowledge was a sign, a kind of "sacrament" of the spiritual fruitfulness that was to come to Adam and Eve in fulfilling their own particular destiny and in the generation of spiritually endowed offspring. Taking it against God's will, Adam and Eve brought death into the world.

The Second Eve, Our Lady, reversed the course of our race by her obedience. Trusting in God's word, she sought only in his will, and in nothing apart from it, the power that would make her fruitful. And the Holy Spirit touched her innermost, most secret being to divine fertility. In Mary the Passover, the Paschal victory, was complete. In Our Lady her divine Son had the perfect tabernacle, the perfect witness and the perfect contemplative.

In this spirit of openness and inner docility we move towards contemplative prayer by a great and simple charity towards all; by the self-denial which is indispensable; by Christ-centered prayer that is a repeated, meditative, murmuring of the name of Jesus in a heart emptied of cares and of images; by a recollection that is a habitual listening for God's command in everything that touches us—all leading forward towards that prayer which "is a yearning for the simple presence of God, for a personal understanding of his word, for knowledge of his will and for capacity to hear and obey him."[8] Where God grants the gift, the contemplative is one who "would rather not know than know. Rather not enjoy than enjoy. Rather not have *proof* that God loves him. He accepts the love of God on faith, in defiance of all apparent evidence. This is the necessary condition for the mystical experience of the reality of God's presence and of his love for us."[9] There we encounter and experience God in what saints have called "the bright obscurity," the "luminous dark."

[1] *Mystics and Zen Masters* (New York: Farrar, Straus and Giroux, 1967), pp. 13–14, 20.

[2] Ibid., pp. 33–34.

[3] Ibid., pp. 25–26.

[4] Thomas Merton *Contemplative Prayer* (New York: Herder and Herder, 1969), pp. 118–119.

[5] *Ascent of Mount Carmel*, II, 4–6.

[6] St. John Chrysostom preached on the incomprehensibility of God at Antioch in 386.

[7] Merton, *Contemplative Prayer*, pp. 105–106.

[8] Ibid., p. 82.

[9] Ibid., p. 111.

IV

Service-Orientated

CHAPTER 15

Mutual Tolerance

In times of war the troops are inescapably committed to fighting shoulder to shoulder for survival and the victory of their side. In times of rapid change which destroys deeply rooted ways and attitudes and seems to threaten the whole way of life of a society, its members may feel themselves embattled. A defensive reaction on the part of some is as inevitable as the feeling of rebellion in others. The defensiveness may be due to emotional attachment to the past; it may also be the consequence of the fearsome vacuum which is created when the old values by which the society's culture was anchored have been swept away and no new values have come into being to take their place. Hence the future is unknown, and the fear which the unknown normally produces is intensified in our day because the changes are proceeding at a pace that is beyond the normal rate of social evolution. "The old myths and symbols by which we oriented ourselves are gone, anxiety is rampant; we cling to each other and try to persuade ourselves that if we choose one thing or one person we'll lose the other, and we are too insecure to take that chance."[1]

Today all the institutions of our society—social, political religious—are being challenged. The technology which was once our great source of strength seems out of control. The result is a widespread sense of helplessness and frustration among the people. How many have the inner resources to resist what

so deeply influences themselves and those around them? The
timid and insecure tend to withdraw and, despite their resentments, become resigned and even apathetic. The aggressive tend
towards loud protest and violence. Now in this matter of violence: the refusal to get involved at the sacrifice of personal
comfort is quite different from nonviolence for the sake of Christ.
Nevertheless, "Anyone who, for a just cause, uses methods
of violence runs the risk not only of perishing 'by the sword'
but also of becoming himself a victim of hatred and injustice,
thus increasing the amount of hatred in the world."[2]

Ultimately, any healthy changes in society and religious culture must have their source in changes in man himself. What
is to guide our thinking today through the labyrinth of personal
convictions, feelings, aims, as we react to the manifold pressures
of our environment?

Polarization in our society is inevitable. Who can say what
is most decisive in our choice of a particular side on which
to stand? Is it, as it should be among Christians, a clearsighted
vision of Christ—who he is, how his message applies to our
times—and a firm will to take our stand at his side for justice,
truth, and love? Does the Sermon on the Mount come through
to us as a movement away from legalism, minimalism, and
adherence to the status quo and towards fulfillment of man's
deepest richness of being through the attainment of the full
stature of the new man as he is in Christ? Does fulfilling the
perennial truth of the Old Testament clearly urge the Christian
to seek that peace for all which is the working out of justice
in full harmony with God's order? Is there an equal concern
for the spiritual tranquility that is Christ's gift to those who
take him seriously and keep his word?

In the matter of necessary change in the Church and in the
conduct of the Christian life: have we a healthy openness to
reasonable and responsible experiment? Or do our insecurities
and anxieties keep us always on the defensive, so that we assume
a posture of blind rigidity; indulge in purple rhetoric and name-
calling with respect to people who are trying their best—even
to the point of alienating and ostracizing those who dare to
differ from us in thought and action? How often does our fear

of the unknown and unpredictable block the friendly interest we should take in the activities of others? How often do we take personality differences, mistakes, and excesses as excuses for rejecting outright an apostolate with solid backing and clear possibilities for great good?

These questions and others like them can serve to test our capacity to distinguish between accidentals and essentials, between appearances and realities, between personality traits and the persons themselves, who are to be respected and loved. They are a way of testing our capacity for openness and genuine tolerance.

But they are not a substitute for authentic love of people just as they are, the love which refuses to judge anyone before God. Apart from exceptional circumstances when a contrary decision must be made either for the good of the individual concerned or that of the Christian community, the love that is a keeping of Christ's word quickly rejects a critical attitude. This is true, partly because criticism gives a feeling of superiority to the critic and partly because a critical attitude creates emotional barriers to sociability and cooperation. Only humble love makes possible the open, nonjudgmental attitude essential to tolerance and mutual concern.

Without this practice of humble love for one another, how can Christians possibly hope that the world will know that they are followers of Jesus? (Jn 13:35). Without mutual tolerance and nonjudgmental acceptance of one another, how can Christians achieve that unity in love, like unto the unity of Father and Son, which is the sign that the Father has sent his Son to be our Savior and that Jesus is present and active among us? (Jn 17:22-23). How otherwise than through mutual love can Christians live up to the friendship that Jesus offers as a pure gift to focus all our relationships with him; his friends, whom the Father loves as he loves his Son? (Jn 15:15). Without a delicate sensitivity to the real person that each one is, whom they see, how can Christians be sensitive to murmuring of the invisible Spirit who dwells in their hearts?

A major hindrance to friendly tolerance and a nonjudgmental attitude is our failure really to forgive those who have offended us. Some of us manage, at times with great effort, to forgive with mind and will. If that is all we can force ourselves to do at a given moment, God does not ask more. But in spite of our brave efforts, feelings of resentment can remain deep down for many years afterwards and unconsciously create barriers of intolerance. In this case we are not really free, nor shall we be until human and spiritual growth permit the Holy Spirit to pour into our hearts the love of God and men that sweeps all barriers away. At that point we must say deliberately that we forgive specifically and totally the persons against whom we have held resentments. Only then shall we have truly surmounted our difficulty and be free.

There are people who are bound in a straightjacket of fears, too rigid to move; yet they would be afraid to live without its support. They cannot admit a new idea, attitude, or manner of living and acting into their shaky world. They feel a terrible need to know all the answers and be absolutely right—hence their resistance to anything which would shake any of their convictions. More than they know, they are motivated by fear of the pain change brings. Perhaps part of this is a fear of being invaded, intruded upon; of having to adjust to another, whether a friend, a co-worker, or just someone in need. So they show extreme concern for protective justice, because they have never experienced the liberation of authentic love. Not having experienced real love, they have little possibility of giving to others the love that makes forgiveness easy: and so when they must forgive it costs them dearly. Yet forgiveness is an essential step to tolerance.

When people feel themselves to be worthless and unlovable, they are unable to believe in any real way that God can forgive them and heal them, either directly or through others. Therefore neither do they believe that others can regard them with compassion, tolerance, and love. So they permit their relationships with others to be corroded by distrust and resentment; they are too cautious to love. They live in the shadows and seldom smile. It is one thing to repress a smile so that superficiality may be avoided, and quite another to be perpetually sad though lack of faith and hope and love.

If we do not believe, with the fullness of faith, that Jesus is the Lord, we shall not be able to realize our responsibility to him and to others in this matter of forgiveness. We shall not realize the extent to which we ourselves are in need of forgiveness; we shall not take Jesus at his word when he says: "If you forgive the faults of others, your heavenly Father will forgive you yours. If you do not forgive others, neither will your Father forgive you" (Mt 6:14). We all need to be forgiven and brought to inner peace through reconciliation with God and with our fellow men. And we have a mutual responsibility for one another: "All of us fall short in many respects" (Jas 3:2). "Every one of you who judges another is inexcusable. By your judgment you convict yourself, since you do the very same things" (Rom 2:1).

With such understanding of ourselves, we will be more understanding and tolerant of other people. But understanding goes much deeper than that. In our natural makeup we differ in the matter of size, strength, coordination, general health. Men and women differ in their responses; men and women differ among themselves in all the elements which enter into one's personal constitution. This calls for the kind of love of one another which looks below the surface and beyond the moment.

We differ from one another in our family formation, in education, in the imprint we have received from the neighborhood in which we grew up. All this must be taken into account in the understanding we give to one another, in our mutual tolerance of differing opinions, approaches, and evaluations.

Besides, is there anyone who is entirely the same from day to day? We are all subject to changes in our physical or emotional condition, to differing pressures and stresses, defeats and successes, to the experience of acceptance or rejection in personal contacts from day to day. And so there must be a day-to-day, indeed even an hour-to-hour, appraisal of one another if we are going to communicate with one another and be mutually supportive and tolerant.

But tolerance goes beyond forgiveness and understanding. We must learn to accept the many different ways in which people hide what is going on inside them and show the compassion which lets them know that they really do not need the mask they wear, since we accept and love them just as they are. There may be many reasons why they are afraid to be themselves. Our only concern must be to bear with them, for the time being, offering them reassurance by our acceptance until they become able to accept themselves, the divinely created selves that are God's glory. This calls for a God-given patience on our part, especially in the beginning when the inner suffering caused by change and rebirth may express itself in stubborn withdrawal, negative attitudes, or even aggressive hostility. It is doubly difficult because all the while our own love is being tested; we are being tried as to our capacity to continue being friendly and calmly supportive in the face of rejection. In any case, we have God's clear directive: "Render true judgement, and show kindness and compassion toward each other" (Zec 7:9).

Would anyone claim the capacity to be consistently tolerant and compassionate without God's special help? We need the Holy Spirit's healing of our own infirmities—our personal fears, our self-preoccupation—as well as the insights he gives us into others. He stands ready to give us this spiritual help most especially when we are trying to serve others. "With your counsel you guide me, and in the end you will receive me in glory" (Ps 73:24). "The wisdom from above is first of all innocent. It is also peaceable, lenient, docile, rich in sympathy and the kindly deeds that are its fruits, impartial and sincere" (Jas 3:17).

Long before Jesus handed himself over to the death he died for us, Jesus lived a life of patient tolerance and compassion that can be appreciated only if we remember the sensitiveness of his perfect manhood. He was not less capable of suffering humanly for being divine. What he taught he lived.

If the standards expressed in the Beatitudes seem austere, it is because the light they shed on our human condition is too strong for our weakened vision. If Jesus seemed to demand too much of human weakness, it was because he knew what human strength would be when it became the open channel of divine power. He was offering us the divine truth, power, and life to fortify us against the inner tendencies which betray our finest human capacities when we let them. If in the standards he set for us Our Lord seemed to disregard how difficult it is for imperfect people to live in an imperfect world, it was his divine wisdom teaching us the meaning of life and of all the circumstances which expose our frailty and wear down our patience. He was teaching the lesson we must always keep relearning—that the way to the order in which peace consists is to keep first things first. "Is not life more than food? Is not the body more valuable than clothes?" (Mt 6:25).

Jesus himself lived in very truth the compassion that is the basis of all tolerance. Moreover, his mercy was a counterculture—something new, fresh, original, and historically important.

In the ancient world, human philosophy had reached its summit in Greece. Greek philosophers talked and wrote about the dignity of man, but the fact was that most of the people of ancient Greece were slaves, who might be branded like animals, sold, or killed by their masters.

In Palestine the Pharisees called themselves the party of the people. Yet they burdened the people with impossible rituals of external purification, legal sinlessness, and religious practice which they themselves did not observe. On top of that, Palestine was an occupied country, and military occupation served the interests of the conqueror rather than of the conquered.

Jesus, by contrast, practiced what he preached. Although he was of royal descent, he served his neighbors at Nazareth as a carpenter. He got specifications for what they wanted made, talked prices with them; made their tables, cabinets, plows, and so on, the way they asked him to. In his public ministry, although his first concern was with spiritual healing and salvation, he was also full of compassion for bodily suffering and healed great numbers of sufferers.

While Jesus was still in the world he chose men to govern his visible community, but he also raised women from their condition of social degradation to great dignity by stressing the primacy of goodness, by accepting the companionship of the women who traveled about with him and his disciples to provide for their material needs. Above all he, God's Son, in choosing a human mother, made a woman the Mother of God.

It was part of Our Lord's tolerance that he never seemed

shocked by sin. Rather, he seemed surprised to find so much goodness. He "showed amazement" at the humility of the centurion who said, "Sir, I am not worthy to have you under my roof. Just give an order and my boy will get better" (Mt 8:8). "I assure you, I have not found this much faith in Israel" (Mt 8:10). He was full of sympathy for the difficulties of poor people. On one occasion he saw a poor widow put two small copper coins into the great Temple treasury. "He called his disciples over and told them: 'I want you to observe that this poor widow contributed more than all the others who donated to the treasury. They gave from their surplus wealth, but she gave from her want, all that she had to live on'" (Mk 12:43-44).

When the crowds acclaimed Jesus as he entered Jerusalem on Palm Sunday and the Pharisees asked him to rebuke his disciples, Jesus said, "If they were to keep silence, I tell you the very stones would cry out" (Lk 19:40). From the very beginning Our Lord paid us the compliment of insisting on the truth. And so the compassionate tolerance he showed for those who "were lying prostrate from exhaustion, like sheep without a shepherd" (Mt 9:36) must always be kept in balance with the Beatitudes and the Sermon on the Mount. He knew our situation, yes; but he neither taught nor exemplified the "situational ethics" whereby man is conceived as the victim of his circumstances; whereby the Christian is forced by circumstances, within or without, to do as others do.

The truth Jesus told us made it clear that we would have to choose to follow him even at considerable human cost. The import of the Beatitudes is that Christianity has to be lived by imperfect human beings among other imperfect human beings in a disturbed world. Sometimes Christians must expect even hatred and persecution. For just such times Jesus said, "What I am doing is sending you out like sheep among wolves. You must be clever as snakes and innocent as doves" (Mt 10:16).

There will be times when it is difficult to know how the principle of tolerance applies: whether it means listening in silence or speaking out boldly and calmly, insisting on what is true and what is right. We need to live consistently in harmony with God's will and habitually alert to the leading of the Holy

Spirit. "When the hour comes, you will be given what you are to say. You yourselves will not be the speakers; the Spirit of your Father will be speaking in you" (Mt 10:19-20).

But we must add realistically that the greatest tolerance and compassion and the most consistent and sincere service to people's real needs do not guarantee that the truth will receive a perfect response. Pharisees and scribes came to Jesus to criticize him. Publicans and sinners came to listen and be converted. We have to accept the difference between ministering to non-believers and to believers. "Into whatever city you go, after they welcome you, eat what they set before you, and cure the sick there. Say to them, 'The reign of God is at hand.' If the people of any town you enter do not welcome you, go into its streets and say, 'We shake the dust of this town from our feet as testimony against you. But know that the reign of God is near' " (Lk 10:8-10).

This is a way of saying that the practice of tolerance has to be kept in proportion by a humble recognition of human limits, our own and others'; by accurate knowledge and clear thinking; and, above all, by that genuine respect and love for people which does not judge but only offers the service which will open up for them the way to helping themselves and to seeking divine help in what is beyond their own limits.

[1] Rollo May, *Love and Will* (New York: Norton, 1969) pp. 13–14.

[2] Bernard Haring, *A Theology of Protest* (New York: Farrar, Straus and Giroux, 1970), pp. 16, 17.

CHAPTER 16

Active Listening
in Human Encounter

Closely related to the service we render one another through mutual tolerance is that which we render by being totally present to another who is endeavoring to communicate with us. Without active listening, communication is impossible.

This may seem a belaboring of the obvious, but actually it is the statement of a crucial need which often goes unrecognized. How often do we tend to listen with half an ear—or less? How often, observing two people supposedly conversing, do we see that the one who is not speaking at the moment has a far-away look in his eyes and is all too ready to be distracted by the most insignificant happening around him? And then, when he does reply to what has been said, his contribution to the conversation has only the vaguest relation to the subject under discussion. How often has the conversation, indeed, become an exchange of monologues rather than any true exchange of thoughts and feelings? Or, worse still, a game of darts in which people use one another as targets for their well-turned phrases, with no regard for the offense which they may be giving one another?

There is scarcely any need to stress the harm which such discourtesy does. One recalls the depth of meaning contained in Newman's observation in his *Idea of a University*: "It is almost a definition of a gentleman to say that he is one who never inflicts pain.'' There is no trait more telling, with regard to anyone's essential personality, than his capacity or incapacity to listen.

But the damage goes deeper than that inflicted upon the social standards of civilized man: it involves the denial to an individual of a spiritual need; it involves the loss to the community of the unique contribution which the individual is capable of making.

The individual needs to be accepted and received not only for what he is but for what he says and does because both spring from what he is. This does not mean that we necessarily agree with a person's views or actions. But the fact is that often, when what he is proposing is either untrue or uncalled for, he himself may be the first to reject it after he has been permitted to express himself and think it through. Or he may be helped towards such a rejection by a sympathetic question which, while it contains no hint of rejection, yet serves to clarify his thought. We all tend to identify with our own ideas and plans, and so any opposition to them is felt as a threat to us personally. The reaction inevitably is defensive resistance.

Actually, a person is not so much concerned with our agreement as with our acceptance of his need to feel the way he does about his ideas and attitudes. The important thing in our personal relations is a total permissiveness that allows an individual to speak freely and openly of what is deep inside him, without any threat of interruption. When we break in on what he is trying to say, it may be precisely at a crucial point of growth, when something very deeply felt is seeking expression. Our interruption may render further development of his thought impossible. And opposition at this point, whether open or only implied, could have a still more inhibiting effect. Indeed, if we do not bring this total permissiveness to our human encounters, we shall not really get to know who a person is—what his orientation to life is, his motivations and his possibilities for growth and achievement. Seen in this light, a failure to listen attentively could be inhumanly cruel, and this is something which needs to be spelled out in its stark truth.

What the individual suffers owing to his lack of growth, the community suffers. For just as the community profits from capacities for service developed by the mature individuals in it, so it undergoes deprivation when the locked-up riches of its members are deprived of development and expression. Hence the responsibility of the community to create an atmosphere of permissive listening which will foster the maximum growth of the individual, not only for the individual's sake but for its own.

Perhaps before we go any further it would be good to describe more in detail what is meant by active listening. Obviously it is much more than having both ears open. It begins with an attitude of mind towards the human person, with the reverence we have stressed in the foregoing chapters. A man's right to be heard out does not come from any qualification such as education, position, or achievement; rather, it is determined by his immeasurable worth as a human person and by the service we owe him.

A total hearing includes much more than the words a person says. We need all the concentration of our being, completely open, with all we can bring to the person and the moment, to listen not only to what the person is saying but also, on another level of consciousness, to why he is saying it; to what he is feeling and why he is feeling it. That is our total person responding to the total person of another. If we listen with any lesser degree of completeness, we are missing something—missing, perhaps, the most important part of the interpersonal communication. And the other person, on his side, has an obscure sense of frustration and rejection. He has not grown; we have not grown. What is involved here is our total consent to be present and responsive to the real person as we find him at this moment. At some other moment he may be different from what he is now, call for a different response from us: our whole concentration must be on the present.

It would have an immensely stimulating effect on human relations if such active and total listening could become a common practice, but the fact is that we can expect it from others only to the extent that we give it. Moreover, neither they nor we

will always be capable of it; none of us can be at our best all
the time. But at least we know what to aim at if we·are going
to come anywhere near the mark.

In any case, only by the cultivation of such openness towards
one another shall we become capable of real discussions in which
each participant grows organically and surely through the
authentic maturing of ideas, feelings, and attitudes. Such an
approach is also the antidote to that jagged, jigsaw kind of conversation in which, though there is interest in the subject on
the part of each speaker, there is no respectful and leisurely
waiting of either for the other to finish what he is saying; but
rather a nervous half-listening, and a nervous waiting for the
first chance·to jump in (or even to break in) with contradictions
or things said off the top of the head. The result is tension
on both sides and a great waste of mental and emotional energy
which produces little light and growth.

Such jigsaw conversations are often the unhappy reflection
of insecurity or vanity on the part of the individuals involved.
Partly, it means that they are more concerned with ideas than
with people, and in this engagement the precious human person
ends up subordinated to a thing, a conversation piece. Partly
it means that they are living out and dramatizing their own
ideas, with which they have identified themselves, and each
is using the other to reflect his own superior image.

In the final analysis, the purpose of conversing is not so much
to give our own answers to another person's questions, but
rather to help him to work out his own answers. Indeed, unless
we have some essential piece of information to impart, we should
avoid giving answers. This requires humility and unselfishness,
for it is always tempting to be momentarily enthroned as a Solo-
mon who pronounces judgment and exudes wisdom. But it is
a temptation to be resisted both for the other's sake and for
our own.

All sincere questioning is an opening up of a person to the
light of truth. It is at once a desire and an opportunity for growth.
(We leave aside for the moment the kind of questioning which,
though sincere enough perhaps, arises from insecurity or a tendency towards dependence.) Active listening concerns itself with

a person's potentiality and desire for growth. A question reveals depths of meaning and feeling, invites the listener to join in a search leading onto sacred ground which is to be approached with reverence. In these depths is the real person; and our first concern is to help the questioner to discover more of himself through the revelation of himself, and to become aware of the strides of growth he is making and where they are leading him. A question rightly received and responded to is the beginning of an adventure; an adventure in which the listener must hold himself in silent reverence before the vista of heights and depths and immeasurable distances opening up before the other person.

The fruit of active listening is the emergence of truth; not truth for its own sake but truth that is the revelation of a person and of the Holy Spirit working in him. This does not mean that it will necessarily be what we think of as a lofty truth, or even a positive one. Indeed, it may be something quite unflattering. But it is just as important to know what we are not as to know what we really are. It is just as important to know our weakness and limits as to know our strength and possibilities. Both together are the truth of what we are, the reality with which we live, work, and communicate with others. We need to know our limits in order to keep within them and so make the most of our capabilities without wasting time and energy on what is beyond us. We need to know our weaknesses in order not to impose them on other people—or, worse still, to communicate them to other people, leading them to be like us in these respects. Such self-knowlege is not loss, though we may feel as if we had lost something; it is not regression but a going forward in hope, with a realistic openness, to make the most of each opportunity. The consequence is a calm acceptance of oneself and peace with God and men. It is not a devaluing of oneself but an affirming of true value that strengthens one's capacity to persevere even in the face of the rejection of our ideas and our plans.

Still another fruit of active listening in human encounter is the enrichment of our own ideas through which we learn from others. Each opening up of ourselves, each revelation of something deep inside ourselves, is at once an act of trust and of love. We love and trust another enough to give him our confidence. He reciprocates our love and trust in daring to disclose something deep in himself to us. His response encourages us to make further self-revelations. So the exchange goes deeper and deeper, and a bond of fellowship and community is forged. This is rarely possible without the help of the Holy Spirit, and it is surely facilitated by his presence and his power.

In any event, the interchange proceeds on the simple awareness that nobody has a monopoly of the truth and that the one truth has many and varied aspects. Even the one aspect which seems to emerge for us may need some clarification through dialogue. Then, by what we see unfolding in another, we are enriched with dimensions of truth hitherto unglimpsed by us. Through the mutual enrichment a happy sense of mutual indebtedness grows, mutual understanding is deepened, and the human community is strengthened.

Eager though we are to obtain such precious fruits as those yielded by active listening, we must begin by looking realistically at the obstacles in our way. Happily, there need be little concern about social pressures, though an environment in which people are given to shouting at each other and constantly interrupting would certainly hinder our practice of respectful listening. We may encounter real environmental difficulties; yet the responsibility for developing our capacity for listening is chiefly ours and the main obstacles are within ourselves.

The greatest block is always fear—fear which exaggerates, or even invents difficulties and saps our courage and initiative. This fear is often deeply related to our self-image, our idea of self, of what we are to accomplish and how we are to establish ourselves in relation to others. Thus, an excessive fear of being thought passive, negative, empty of positive ideas, not really interested in people—a fear of being left out, regarded as a nobody—can precipitate us into talking too much and interrupting when we should be respectfully and actively listening. As we have already noted, we tend to identify ourselves with our ideas and plans and feel that any threat to them is a threat to our very being.

There is, moreover, our fear of disagreement: this should have no place in active listening, for it should be realized that unity of hearts can be achieved and strengthened without, necessarily, a full unanimity of minds. The consensus needed for effective common action does not require complete agreement of minds so long as there is a willingness to cooperate. Diversity in unity and unity in diversity permit the free action of the Holy Spirit through the distinctive gifts of each person.

Nevertheless differences of various kinds do challenge a person's capacity to listen actively and profoundly to another. How far is he capable of remaining present to and embracing in this total response precisely the differences which make the other person what he is? By this we mean the manifold factors which enter into the constitution of this individual—physical, emotional, educational; hereditary and environmental; the modifications derived from private reading, personal experience, friendships, and so on. These natural elements in the personality color what the person is doing and saying at any given moment, for there will be differences in the knowledge of facts as well as some differences in principles or in the way principles are interpreted. There will be crucial differences in the way the person uses words, which may confuse the most perceptive listener. But it is the person who matters: the precious human person remains the unchanging core from which every aspect of his personality emanates and to which our most attentive listening must reach.

The person who listens perceptively must make it a matter of special concern that in any spontaneous interchange it is rare for a speaker to express himself completely and well when he is talking about something for the first time, all the more if it is something deep inside him. He is likely to say only part of what he means; or he may say it unclearly, or indeed so badly that he ends up giving an impression which is the opposite of what he intends. Therefore it is essential, in listening actively, not to contradict when someone says what may be, or may seem to be, wrong. What is needed is a simple question or a sympathetic silence that will give him a chance to try again to say what he really means and to express the full meaning of what he intends.

If we are to listen perceptively and actively, we shall find ourselves put to a severe test in that we shall have to re-examine our own image of people—what we expect of them in relation to ourselves and others, to their life work, to community living, to God. For we tend to expect people to speak and act according to the image we have formed of them and hence to interpret what they are saying in accordance with that image. How much is there in us of the finger-shaking teacher whose voice takes on an edge when an opinion is expressed which is in opposition to his own—and thus threatens, he feels, something very deep in himself?

How aware are we of the extent to which our personal experience and personal feelings tilt our thinking and our attitudes, contributing to the difficulty we have in being calmly objective in listening sensitively and openly to another? How aware are we of the way even the matter of a physical constitution different from our own may produce a difference in the way the other person thinks and feels about things? How ready are we to overcompensate for the differences between us by way of sympathy, rather than risk prejudging or misinterpreting what is said?

Only by facing the barriers to sensitive and active listening realistically can we realize the demands it makes on us. Only then shall we be able to prevent those barriers from creating in us the emotional disturbance which closes little doors in the mind and draws defensive lines against the threat of invasion or against demands beyond our capacity to meet. Unquestionably, we are required to achieve a great warm tolerance that can afford to be open precisely because it is so firmly grounded in a clear recognition of what is real. This calls for a humble self-confidence that is willing to be and let be, to live and let live; to give the same freedom to the thought and feeling of others that we wish for our own. This is the way to that unfolding of inner resources which reveals the gifts of God to the human person and puts those gifts at the service of all.

Needless to say, the very exacting requirements of active listening in our human encounters suggest our need of the gifts of the Holy Spirit, both to activate our natural gifts and to enable us to go beyond them in our understanding and our response to others. We have his commitment to be with us in creating unity in love, and where more certainly than in our service of the obvious needs of others? "Rejoice with those who rejoice," says Rom 12:15, "weep with those who weep."

Our modern world has developed a variety of techniques to serve the psychological needs of our fellow men at every level of life—sensitivity training, pastoral counseling, client-centered therapy. The basis of them all is precisely the perceptiveness and response involved in active listening. We learn from this how indispensable is this service rendered to others in daily life. Far more importantly, we learn the need of a Christ-centered approach to people, and the wisdom of his way: "Learn from me, for I am gentle and humble of heart" (Mt 11:29).

CHAPTER 17

Service through Supportive Teamwork

Throughout history the two great forces of good and evil have always been at work, always present together, always in conflict with each other. From time to time the tension between the two seems to break, and one seems to advance and the other to recede. In our day we are experiencing this tension very strongly, and the result is a suffering which bites deep into the heart of our being.

But as we have already said, at least in our time we are becoming increasingly aware that the individual cannot stand alone against forces of such magnitude as the forces of evil in our world; the individual cannot alone carry forward the forces for good which are represented by everything that is right and positive. We recognize the need of cooperation in community under clear-sighted leadership. We know that instead of witnessing to evil by lamentation and despair we have to seek out truth and goodness, unite with those who share a vision of hope, strengthen our faith and joy in God's presence and power among us, and support the leadership of those who are God's prophetic instruments.

When Jesus formed the nucleus of the new Christian community he tried to reduce conflicts to the minimum and ensure the maximum of fellowship and cooperation by choosing men who were both mature and accustomed to working together, some of them blood brothers—Peter, Andrew, John, James, and

Jude—and others close friends—John and Peter, Philip, and Nathanael (later Bartholomew). But there was considerable variety in their social backgrounds. Whereas the first chosen were fishermen, Philip seems to have been at home in merchandising and Judas Iscariot in administration. Their intellectual persuasions ranged from those of Simon the Zealot to those of Matthew the Herodian government official. Rivalries and strong feelings about power and position soon developed (Mk 10:37). The leadership of Jesus and the inner conversion wrought by the baptism of the Holy Spirit were needed to weld these disciples into the college of apostles.

Like the apostles, the Christian community needs the goals set by Jesus through his life, accomplishments, and message. These goals reach to the depths of our being, to the heights of heaven to which we are called and to the breadth of the world through which we move on pilgrimage. Our Christian path leads us not away from trouble but straight into its midst, always where we are needed most.

The very magnitude of our Christian undertaking can draw us on and on, deeper and deeper into ceaseless activity, as if we were the sole initiators of a commitment that had to be carried forward to completion all by ourselves. Actually, we only take up where others have left off and carry on for our own brief span; others take up our unfinished task, carrying forward in their time the continuous work of redemption which goes on until the end of time. For this reason prudence demands that we should have regular withdrawals in rest and prayer to replenish our resources and refocus our thinking.

To keep our goals clear, we have to see ourselves as part of the whole Christian undertaking, deeply committed to it, but always within the human limits that come to focus in prayer. In prayer we shall be assisted in making the prudent choice of where we can best function at the moment.

But in our prayer a very delicate balance must be maintained if a certain danger is to be avoided: namely, that the very focus which clarifies our human limitations and recalls our personal infidelities may fill us with a sense of emptiness and dread from which we want to escape into more activity, especially "good" activity. Always we must weigh against our sense of human limitation our confidence in the biblical commitment of God to give us his power and love in the Holy Spirit. While authentic dependence on God is attended by a happy confidence in his complete control of the world, we need also to live and work in the joyous confidence that Jesus has given us the full power to carry out in the world the work of salvation which he achieved for all men on the cross. We need to keep constantly in mind that some measure of the redemption is achieved through each life rightly lived by New Testament norms and through each individual or community effort to love, serve, and bear witness to Christ.

What matters is that God made his covenant with the Christian community, and through the community with the individual. This means that what is required of each member of the community is the acceptance of himself, the confidence that God chooses to use him just as he is, even while God keeps drawing him to open himself still more completely to the divine presence, friendship, power, and life. Only with everyone centering his confidence in God, and not in his merely natural self, can there be the confidence between the members of the community which facilitates God's work. Self-confidence increases our capacity for trusting others and working with them, but in the long run the essential thing in all community effort, as in all true friendship, is the direction towards goals which are beyond the objectives of the individuals personally, beyond the scope of the community itself and larger than either. We need a mystery of unknown reaches and depths in which to immerse ourselves, a mystery in which our human helplessness loses its meaning and we are lifted to heights of achievement which exceed all our calculations. We need a fellowship in the Holy Spirit which binds us ever more securely, without our knowing why or how, in a unity that holds firm, resisting the contagion of evil.

All our service to our fellow men, even in the power given to us individually and through the community, must still embrace the Christian paradoxes. ''We are called impostors, yet we are truthful; nobodies who in fact are well known; dead, yet we are alive; punished, but not put to death; sorrowful, though we are always rejoicing; poor, yet we enrich many. We seem to have nothing, yet everything is ours!'' (2 Cor 6:8-10). Our effectiveness in witnessing to Christ and ministering to men depends on a firm conviction that it is God who is in control, God who is acting through us as instruments—not because he could not dispense with us but because he chooses to approach men in the least frightening way, through their fellow men.

Our confidence is precisely in this:

> God's folly is wiser than men, and his weakness more powerful than men. . . . God chose those whom the world considers absurd to shame the wise; he singled out the weak of this world to shame the strong. He chose the world's low-born and despised, those who count for nothing, to reduce to nothing those who are something; so that mankind can do no boasting before God. God it is who has given you life in Christ Jesus. He has made him our wisdom and also our justice, our sanctification, and our redemption. (1 Cor 1:25, 27-30)

With this in view we shall see that we have no need to preoccupy ourselves with our self-image, no need to be on the defensive for fear of being treated as a nobody. Baptized in Christ, we share his friendship and his power. Conscious of our spiritual worth and riches, we are more at ease in respecting those we serve.

We should also keep in mind the many ways in which our fellow men serve us, and this includes the ones who need us at the moment. They too are serving our needs, especially the need to be needed.

This attitude is the antidote to that sense of superiority which is so likely to poison any sort of "do-goodism." It also forestalls both the fear of being dependent on other people and the resentment which tends to arise when such dependence exists. Our service is founded in respect, and through the dependence our love is deepened. In the last analysis, the mark of genuine charity is that it is recognized, and responded to, as love which needs to serve.

What we said above in Chapter 1 about adaptability in working out group decisions and responsibility in carrying them into effect applies especially here. Since there are so many ways to serve and many of them very good, group work requires a mature adaptability in dividing the work and disciplining oneself to do it well, cheerfully, and cooperatively. At times there will be confidential information about the need or the persons involved which justice to them will not permit to be divulged, not even to one who comes to minister to them in the name of the Lord. Excessive curiosity has no place in Christian charity.

Whatever the conditions in which we pull together in any enterprise, our relationship to others must involve a great loyalty. This means a practical loyalty. Loyalty is not a vague sentiment diffused over a group, it is in the first instance always a person-to-person relationship. Group loyalty is welded between individuals. The warmth of group loyalty is something spreading from person to person, and any failure of loyalty towards an individual injures the whole group. So also does any exclusiveness in friendship which leaves some members out.

We can never forget that unity in love is a sign that Jesus is our Savior and that the Father loves us as he loves his Son. St. Paul rebuked the Corinthians for taking their disputes into pagan courts, thus giving scandal. "You yourselves injure and cheat your very own brothers. Must brother drag brother into court, and before unbelievers at that?" (1 Cor 6:8, 6). Indeed, it was appalling to him that these new Christians should have lawsuits at all: such divisions and disloyalty should at all costs be avoided.

Are we any better than those new Christians? Lawsuits aside, are we too quick to put another on trial in the court of our human, natural judgments (which so often rest on questionable motives), when we should be leaving the judgment to God and supporting one another loyally so far as we can? "Has Christ been divided into parts?" (1 Cor 1:13).

Even apart from the damage done to group cooperation by disloyalty, it is damaging in the first place to ourselves. When we prove untrustworthy we destroy our own integrity in the eyes of others, but even more particularly in our own. We know this and suffer uneasiness and remorse; we lose the inner peace which comes from keeping our life an open book—the open book of a generous, loyal, and dedicated person. Keeping our integrity in difficult circumstances often requires great courage.

We owe loyalty to one another, finally, in our commitment to community life and service, service to one another within the group and service to others beyond it. We honor that commitment by our own fidelity to everything which helps us to dispose ourselves for receiving God's grace through prayer, penance, charity, and disciplined cooperation with authority. Our constancy and fervor in these things strengthens theirs. It must be remembered that we can never be neutral in our influence on one another: our influence is always either good or bad. This is our exercise of Christ's priesthood and mission towards one another: thus do we support and sanctify one another in our common search for the experience of God.

This need we have of one another's loyalty will be all the more real to us in the measure that we experience times of defeat, confusion, and depression and are aware of the same thing in others. At such times it is a great help to know that we are not going it alone, that we can depend on the loyalty of others not to make it worse and to do what they can to share the burden. This does not mean that we shall feel sorry for ourselves, but there is a loneliness in all real suffering which cannot be shared. The understanding support of others at these times at least helps us bear the suffering and loneliness and to carry on, setting ourselves aside for the sake of those who need us.

Even Our Lord was not entirely alone in his passion and death. On the way to Calvary, as he staggered under the weight of the cross, he had Simon of Cyrene. He had the women of Jerusalem. He had John, the disciple he loved and who loved him. He had his own mother. And he had the good thief who loved justice. In the same way, we should help one another in the carrying of the cross which leads to the resurrection.

Our exercise of loyalty will be a matter of judgment in individual cases. There are times when we shall practice the loyalty of silence—those times when a loyal defense would only provoke further attack and baseless charges are best allowed to be rendered ineffectual by their own untruth. We can be loyally supportive when an open verbal defense of another would help. And we can give each other the loyalty of action by doing everything possible for one another in our common undertakings.

The development of love, loyalty, and the spirit of service in the Christian community, which we have been discussing, requires a quality of leadership that embodies these very goals. Authority has already been described in the chapter on collegiality as constituted to achieve unity of action and to promote the growth of the members of the group towards their goals. Clearly, then, authority is a way of serving the common and the individual good. And in a democratic age, authority is most at home as service. Jesus himself set the example:

> You address me as "Teacher" and "Lord," and fittingly enough, for that is what I am. But if I washed your feet—I who am Teacher and Lord—then you must wash each other's feet. What I just did was to give you an example: as I have done, so you must do. I solemnly assure you, no slave is greater than his master; no messenger outranks the one who sent him. (Jn 13:13-16)

"There is no authority except from God, and all authority that exists is established by God" (Rom 13:1). We are in the final day of salvation, the final age of the world in which all is made new in Christ Jesus. The signs, announcements, and preparations of the Old Testament have become the final realities. Buildings, sacraments, ceremonies, powers, and laws are all secondary and subordinate to men and the divine life within them. "You are the body of Christ. Every one of you is a member of it" (1 Cor 12:27). The sacrifices, priesthood, sabbath, and covenant are all made new in Christ, who is our new and eternal covenant. All reality points to the final victory of Christ in which all power and dominion will be given over to Christ, all pain and hardship will be taken away, all material things will be transformed, and everything will be spiritual and interior.

In this final day of salvation "you have been called to live in freedom—but not a freedom that gives free rein to the flesh. Out of love, place yourselves at one another's service" (Gal

5:13). Christianity is mutual service centered in Christ our God. Everything comes from God for the sake of everybody. The order of authority must not be separated from the order of personal spiritual gifts. Authority is a title and function in its own right, but it is conferred within a general order of service and does not exist outside of it. The dignity and value of the service is measured by the stature of the entire Christian community, which is consecrated, holy, and dedicated to the ministry and to witnessing. "You are 'a chosen race, a royal priesthood, a holy nation, a people he claims for his own to proclaim the glorious works of the One who called you from darkness into his marvelous light' " (1 Pt 2:9). Some are leaders in the service to the others. Their title unites and organizes the service of everyone, making it truly a service of the whole body, a communal ministry.

Hence the entire Christian community has a responsibility for the manner in which authority is exercised, i.e. with respect, cooperation, help, and love, but not with the servility from below that encourages aloofness and domineering from above. All who hold authority are, in turn, responsible to God and to everyone. Authority exists and is exercised only in a fraternal community of service. This concept demands a very profound conversion—not so much to a moral ideal of disinterested service, because that ideal is only the consequence, but a conversion to God, to Christ, the one Lord and one source of all life. All live in Christ for the victory and glory of Christ and for unity and charity among men. Hence, the great need for companionship and mutual service among the members as well as common service and bearing witness beyond the Christian community. "Let us profess the truth in love and grow to the full maturity of Christ the head. Through him the whole body grows, and with the proper functioning of the members joined firmly together by each supporting ligament, builds itself up in love" (Eph 4:15-16).

CHAPTER 18

Serving Christ
and Our Brothers and Sisters

There is a kind of spirituality which is conceived as "service-centered." Its slogan, in recent years, was "God is where the action is!" When it was in its heyday, prayer was downgraded as an escape from the urgent realities of the day. It was above all a time of slogans in which the mind had little role. Happily it seems definitely on the wane now, because people began to experience some of its fruits: physical exhaustion, spiritual and social disorientation which were the consequence of frenetic action with no pause to reflect. Playing the inexhaustible God can be exhilarating for a while, but presently one begins to feel as if one were on an "apostolic" merry-go-round. Above all, when one begins to look around it is hard to add up tangible and enduring accomplishments.

By way of reaction to all this, some people have withdrawn completely from an active apostolate, either unable or unwilling to try again. Others have rightly concluded that any real human and Christian growth must be organic, from within, and at the pace indicated by each distinctive personality, by the signs of the times, and by the word of God. Wisely guided, both humanly and divinely, they have learned to depend less on their own efforts to initiate, carry on, and complete a service of the moment or a continuing apostolate and more on the light and impulse of the Holy Spirit. God is, of course, where the action is; but he is there working through us as instruments. So while these people's lives are no longer service-centered—well-intentioned but weak in faith and prayer—they are still very service-orientated, for they are Christ-centered and Spirit-filled through constant refocusing and renewal in prayer.

The God who centers the universe did not contradict his time-less, eternal nature by saying; "I am who was"; he said, "I am who am." And Jesus said, "I am with you always, until the end of the world" (Mt 28:20). Jesus likewise said, "As you have sent me into the world, so I have sent them into the world" (Jn 17:18). So Christianity, like its eternal Founder, is very much a "now" religion, and every Christian is a "now" Christian, sent to continue what Jesus began. The consummation is not yet, but it is on the way, owing to the apostolate of those who are living with the life of Christ:

> The apostolate is carried on through the faith, hope and charity which the Holy Spirit diffuses in the hearts of all members of the Church. Indeed, the law of love, which is the Lord's greatest commandment, impels all the faithful to promote God's glory through the spread of his kingdom and to obtain for all men that eternal life which consists in knowing the only true God and him whom he sent, Jesus Christ (cf. Jn 17:3). On all Christians therefore is laid the splendid burden of working to make the divine message of salvation known and accepted by all men throughout the world. (Vatican II, Decree on the Apostolate of the Laity, no. 3)

When Jesus said, "I was hungry and you gave me food, I was thirsty and you gave me drink. As long as you did it for one of my least brothers, you did it for me" (Mt 25:35, 40), he was asking us to find him in the needs of others and never to separate him from those in need. That means much more than adoring, loving, and serving Christ in the person, while merely tolerating and perhaps half-ignoring the real person involved. Jesus asks that we see him and the real person we serve in one single faith and love, experience him as one with the person and be enriched and blessed by both. To identify with Christ, we have to identify with the person. "Look on the needs of the saints as your own" (Rom 12:13).

To serve at all is to serve the whole person with the distinctive material, affective, spiritual, and intellectual needs that are the stress of the moment in each one. This total apostolate was the way of Jesus:

> Jesus continued his tour of all the towns and villages. He taught in their synagogues, he proclaimed the good news of God's reign, and he cured every sickness and disease. At the sight of the crowds, his heart was moved with pity. They were lying prostrate with exhaustion, like sheep without a shepherd. He said to his disciples: "The harvest is good but laborers are scarce. Beg the harvest master to send out laborers to gather his harvest." Then he summoned his twelve disciples and gave them authority to expel unclean spirits and to cure sickness and disease of every kind. (Mt 9:35—10:1)

These same powers, Jesus promised, would accompany those who believe:

> Signs like these will accompany those who have professed their faith: they will use my name to expel demons, they will speak entirely new languages, they will be able to handle serpents, they will be able to drink deadly poison without harm, and the sick upon whom they lay their hands will recover. (Mk 16:17-18)

These are the gifts of the Holy Spirit that are given Christians for the common good:

> To each person the manifestation of the Spirit is given for the common good. To one the Spirit gives wisdom in discourse, to another the power to express knowledge. Through the Spirit one receives faith; by the same Spirit another is given the gift of healing, and still another miraculous powers. Prophecy is given to one; to another power to distinguish one spirit from another. One receives the gift of tongues, another that of interpreting tongues. (1 Cor 12:7-10)

The ministry of Jesus was to the whole human person. This total service is what we are to continue, and with all the gifts and powers he places in our hands when we have the faith to receive them and use them as he wills. The way to such faith is a reading and understanding of all that Jesus said and did personally, and through his Holy Spirit. Such faith is rarely achieved except in a Christian community which has both the understanding and the exercise of the gifts. Faith is awakened and strengthened by repeatedly witnessing the operation of God's power through the gifts, until such faith reaches a degree of intensity and confidence that individuals and the community are deeply committed to God in their dependence, their trust in his committed love, and their continuous thanksgiving for this goodness poured out upon them. Tragically, a malformation in the education of an individual or in a whole religious culture can hinder both the understanding and the operation of the gifts that are so clearly indicated in the New Testament but are so seldom preached. "Faith, then, comes through hearing, and what is heard is the word of Christ" (Rom 10:17).

The Second Vatican Council, in spite of the initial opposition of a conservative minority, took an uncompromising lead in encouraging full awareness and right use of these distinct ways of serving the Christian community. In the Decree on the Apostolate of the Laity (no. 3) it declares:

> For the exercise of this apostolate, the Holy Spirit who sanctifies the People of God through the ministry and the sacraments gives to the faithful special gifts as well (cf. 1 Cor 12:7), "allotting to everyone according as he will" (1 Cor 12:11). Thus may the individual, "according to the gift that each has received, administer it to one another" and become "good stewards of the manifold grace of God" (1 Pt 4:10), and build up thereby the whole body in charity (cf. Eph 4:16). From the reception of these charisms or gifts, including those which are less dramatic, there arise for each believer the right and duty to use them in the Church and in the world for the good of mankind and the upbuilding of the Church. In so doing, believers need to enjoy the freedom of the Holy Spirit who "breathes where he wills" (Jn 3:8). At the same time, they must act in communion with their brothers in Christ, especially with their pastors. The latter must make a judgment about the true nature and proper use of these gifts, not in order to extinguish the Spirit, but to test all things and hold fast to what is good (cf. 1 Thes 5:12, 19, 21).

In spite of the use of all the powers given to believers as their "right and duty" and "for the good of mankind," there will always remain untold suffering in the world, in part because of unbelief. It was the same with Jesus at Nazareth. "He could work no miracle there, apart from curing a few who were sick by laying hands on them, so much did their lack of faith distress him" (Mk 6:5-6). Besides, there will always be a place in the scheme of salvation for vicarious suffering. "In my own flesh I fill up what is lacking in the sufferings of Christ for the sake of his body, the church" (Col 1:24). Perhaps the need of vicarious suffering is itself due to unbelief.

In any case, our compassionate service to men must be as broad as that of Jesus. And it is angelism to imagine that Jesus was interested only in the spiritual and supernatural. He honored a wedding celebration by joining his Mother at Cana and by working his first miracle at her suggestion in order to relieve the shortage of wine that embarrassed the young couple; he had compassion on their need.

Once, in the full heat of late summer, when the crowds stayed with him to listen to him preach and to have their sick healed, Jesus said to his apostles, as if asking their advice, "My heart is moved with pity for the crowd. If I send them home hungry, they will collapse on the way. Some of them have come a great distance" (Mk 8:203). Then he miraculously multiplied loaves and fishes to feed the hunger of men, women, and children.

We should not take the quickness to feed the hungry as an accident of circumstances nor merely as an attempt of Our Lord to prove his divinity. In his desert fast Jesus learned from painful experience what extreme hunger was like. His hunger from that fast of forty days and nights was his personal experience of suffering with the hungry of all times and places, including the millions of our own time. Too few of those who are making the decisions that affect the world's millions have ever experienced prolonged hunger. Without such experience it is easy for them to theorize and occupy themselves with other things.

We see Our Lord's understanding of the hunger of his fishermen apostles. After his resurrection, when he appeared to them on the shores of the Lake of Galilee, he knew they were very hungry after a night of wrestling with nets on the lake. And he knew their stomachs seemed all the emptier because their

nets were empty. They had caught nothing. They were discour-
aged. First Jesus revived their spirits by miraculously filling their
nets with fish. Then he, the risen, glorified Lord, prepared a
hot breakfast of bread and fish and served them himself.

In his compassion Jesus let all the blind, crippled, and diseased
of Palestine come to him, like the waves of the sea breaking
over a rock. The prophet Isaiah foretold not only Christ's passion
and death (1 Pt 2:24) but also his compassion for all suffering:
"It was our infirmities that he bore, our sufferings that he
endured" (Is 53:4, Mt 8:17). It still remains true that all the
believer's power to relieve suffering and cure illness comes from
the victory of Christ on the cross.

Most of Christ's miracles of healing seem to have been per-
formed not to prove his divinity to unbelievers but directly out
of compassion, directly from the desire to relieve suffering. It
seems that unbelief, far from calling forth miracles, rather hindered them—as we have remarked with reference to his home
town of Nazareth. It should be abundantly clear to us, therefore,
that we should stimulate in ourselves not only a theoretical
acceptance but a practical belief that Jesus can and still wants
to continue to relieve suffering through us.

Jesus does not demand perfection in believers before he works
through them—much less talent or prestige. In his own time
there was usually enough belief, however weak or misdirected,
to keep Our Lord's goodness flowing out in a flood of compassion. At one point, when challenged by the disciples of the
Baptist, he appealed to his miracles of mercy as an indication
that he was the true Savior foretold by Isaiah (35:5; 61:1; 63:3):

> Go and report to John what you have seen and heard. The blind
> recover their sight, cripples walk, lepers are cured, the deaf hear,
> dead men are raised to life and the poor have the good news
> preached to them. (Lk 7:22)

Even the Gentiles of the Decapolis could see the mercy-
healings as clear signs that here was at least a man of God:

> Large crowds of people came to him bringing with them cripples,
> the deformed, the blind, the mute, and many others besides. They

laid them at his feet and he cured them. The result was great astonishment in the crowds as they beheld the mute speaking, the deformed made sound, cripples walking about, and the blind seeing. They glorified the God of Israel. (Mt 15:3-31)

Besides, there was no distinction in nis miraculous giving. He cured not only his own people but also the daughter of the Syro-Phoenician woman. He raised to life not only his friend Lazarus but also the slave of the garrison captain at Capharnaum.

Less obvious than physical ills but no less painful are the infidelities that devastate our pride and the humiliating tangles we get ourselves into through misjudgment and presumption. Yet for those, also, who fail in this way, our service to men must be like that of Jesus. He was as tender and understanding to the Samaritan woman at the well as he was to the learned Nicodemus of the mighty Sanhedrin. He understood the misguided zeal of James and John, the fiery sons of Zebedee, who wanted to assault the inhospitable Samaritans with fire from heaven, even though he rebuked them for being alien to his spirit and lacking in compassion. Jesus was still tender towards the weary John who could not even pray with him through the moments of his terrible agony. "The spirit is willing but nature is weak" (Mk 14:38).

At another critical moment, during his passion, the compassionate glance of Jesus turned the cowardly Peter into a weeping penitent restored to loyalty to his Lord. "The Lord turned around and looked at Peter, and Peter remembered the word that the Lord had spoken to him, 'Before the cock crows today you will deny me three times!' He went out and wept bitterly" (Lk 22:61-62).

Our service to men needs the all-embracing, compassionate tenderness that Jesus dramatized in the three great parables of the lost sheep, the lost coin, and the prodigal son. The ninety-nine sheep are left in the desert while the search for the lost sheep goes on. And the joy of finding the one lost sheep bursts into the celebration with friends and neighbors. "There will likewise be more joy in heaven over one repentant sinner than over ninety-nine righteous people who have no need to repent"

(Lk 15:7). He was not making a comparison of numbers; he really said nothing about the ninety-nine, except perhaps to suggest their self-righteousness. Working within the limits of language, and using the ninety-nine, Jesus makes a comparison of intensity; he meant only to express the greatness of the joy over the one who repents.

In the third parable the prodigal son resolved to go home to his father and say, "Father, I have sinned against God and against you; I no longer deserve to be called your son. Treat me like one of your hired hands" (Lk 15:18). At that moment he was all of us; for all of us, if only for minor infidelities, are prodigals returning home to God and pleading for mercy. Fortunately for all of us, the mercy of God is there in those lines: "While he was still a long way off, his father caught sight of him and was deeply moved. He ran out to meet him, threw his arms around his neck, and kissed him" (Lk 15:20). That is the spirit we need to prevent any self-righteousness towards a person who is in trouble through his own fault.

It is so easy to ask people to change their ways so that they will not need so much attention. And we have to counsel them as much as we can to take control of themselves and their circumstances. But in the end we must often weep at their unwillingness to wrench themselves free from ways that are deeply rooted in their whole being. In the Sermon on the Mount Jesus tried to tell the people about what was true and false in their thinking and customs. In his own life he lived all that remained true and valid from the Old Testament. But in the end he could only weep over their incredible blindness in not accepting him as their Savior, and over the tragic consequences of their rejection. The city of Jerusalem at once symbolized all his natural love for his country and all his religious loyalty to his Father:

> Coming within sight of the city, he wept over it and said: "If only you had known the path to peace this day; but you have completely lost it from view! Days will come upon you when your enemies encircle you with a rampart, hem you in, and press you hard from every side. They will wipe you out, you and your children within your walls, and leave not a stone on a stone within you,

because you failed to recognize the time of your visitation." (Lk 19:41-44)

We really do not know the human heart of Jesus unless we know the depths of meaning in that passage.

Since the moral tone and culture of any society depends so much on the religious quality of its women, our service to our fellow men must necessarily include a concern for the dignity of women. In the world into which Jesus came, woman was a chattel, useful to man for childbearing and the object of his pleasure. Despite an ethic above that of the surrounding pagan world, woman's position among Jesus' own people was not very much higher. In this sense the Incarnation radically altered the position of woman in history: a woman acquired a dignity possible to no man in becoming the Mother of God. From a uniquely favored woman Christ received human life and human care. In becoming man, Jesus elevated the masculine nature; in his own Mother he elevated the nature of woman. The motherhood of Mary elevates the status of women as long as men and women honor Jesus and his mother.

But Jesus did something more, which was rather daring for a time in which a rabbi in Israel would not so much as speak to a woman in public: he received women openly into his friendship. There were, as we have noted, a number of women who went about with Jesus and the apostles on their journeys:

> After this he journeyed through towns and villages preaching and proclaiming the good news of the kingdom of God. The Twelve accompanied him, and also some women who had been cured of evil spirits and maladies: Mary called the Magdalene, from whom seven devils had gone out, Joanna, the wife of Herod's steward Chuza, Susanna, and many others who were assisting them out of their means. (Lk 8:1-3)

Moreover, Jesus declared that women are spiritually the equal of men when he said, in the hearing of his own mother: "Whoever does the will of my heavenly Father is brother and sister and mother to me" (Mt 12:50). In a society which has in so many respects become pagan, we must ask ourselves whether our attitude towards women is in accordance with Christian norms.

As members of the mystical body of Christ we are more closely related to one another than through any human kinship:

> All of you who have been baptized into Christ have clothed your-selves with him. There does not exist among you Jew or Greek, slave or freeman, male or female. All are one in Christ Jesus. Furthermore, if you belong to Christ you are the descendants of Abraham, which means you inherit all that was promised. (Gal 3:27-29)

In our brothers and sisters in Christ material, emotional, and spiritual needs are so inextricably intertwined that we must approach each person with a nonjudgmental love which seeks to serve one who is delivered, purchased, redeemed "by Christ's blood beyond all price: the blood of a spotless, unblemished lamb" (1 Pt 1:19). The most obvious need, of whatever kind, is the point of entry through which we shall find the whole person, ministering to one need after another, as they reveal themselves, until, God willing, we find Christ working at the core of the person's being. There we adore and love with praise and thanksgiving:

> I sought my soul,
>   but my soul I could not see.
> I sought my God,
>   but my God eluded me.
> I sought my brother—
>   and I found all three.

V

Affective

CHAPTER 19

The Total Person
Involved in the Experience of God

In our time Christian thought is far removed from that excessive
stress upon the rational aspect of man's nature, at the expense
of sense and feeling, which characterized so much of the spirituality of the past. The writer on spiritual subjects is no longer
in need of defending the rightness, indeed the sacredness, of
human emotions. But while these powerful dynamic forces
within us are no longer regarded as a kind of dark morass in
which man finds himself betrayed, we are still far from achieving
a full understanding of their mysterious influences on the entire
human personality and farther still from the balanced mastery
which permits freedom from anxiety, inner peace, and the full
use of the richness of man's inner resources both for serving
others and for achieving his own destiny.

The fact is that even in face of enlightened teaching with
regard to the old puritanism, which was a deformation of Christian truth, modern man remains afflicted with a false sense of
guilt. The attempt is made to resolve this, so far as man's experience of God is concerned, in several ways. First there are those
who, in the effort to avoid being overwhelmed by their sense
of unworthiness, stress the completeness of Christ's redemptive
work. Jesus, they say, has taken all our guilt upon himself.
The total victory is his, and we are to be concerned only with

peace, love, and joy. The implication is that the grace Christ won for us on Calvary *covers* all our sins. But though this partial truth may make man's sense of guilt less unbearable, it cannot remove guilt, it can only disguise it. And what is lost is the reality of man's freedom, in which he is empowered by grace to share, through the yielding of his will to God, in Christ's work of redemption that continues until the end of the world.

At the opposite extreme are those who take Christ's redemptive sacrifice insufficiently into acount. These are the people who sincerely strive to face themselves and are constantly concerned with appeasing God for their infidelities. Very often their idea of God contains too much of the image of the heartless bookkeeper who will not let them rest or even really enjoy themselves without feeling guilty about it. In many cases such individuals have never experienced themselves as lovable owing to the deprivation of affection in childhood. Lacking the image of an earthly father who loves them, they are unable to form the image of a heavenly Father full of loving-kindness. They are unaware of the almighty Savior that Jesus is, and of how the Father is committed to hear every prayer offered in the name of Jesus, including—and especially—a prayer for forgiveness.

Then, of course, there are those who are detached from religious influences, for whom the concepts of sin and guilt belong to a prescientific past. On the conscious level, they are free of the feeling of guilt which afflicts the believer; yet that they are free of the believer's tensions is questionable. For there are elements in our culture which inhibit the right functioning of the very dynamic elements of personality which we have struggled so long to accept and appreciate. As Rollo May says:

> There is in our society a definite trend toward a state of affectlessness as an attitude toward life, a character state . . . Estrangement, playing it cool, alienation, withdrawal of feeling, indifference, anomie, depersonalization—each one of these terms expresses a part of the condition to which I refer . . . This affectlessness is a shrinking-up in the winds of continuous demands, a freezing in the face of hyperstimuli, letting the current go by since one fears he would be overwhelmed if he responded to it. Our tragic

paradox is that in contemporary history, we *have* to protect ourselves by some kind of apathy.[1]

Moreover, whether as an effect of the same social forces which produced the current defensive apathy or as an effect of the apathy itself, there has come, in violation of man's very nature, a reduction to the banal of the tremendous mystery at the heart of man's being: the sacred mating instinct of procreation. Our immediate concern with this is that it results in a further diminution of man's affective sensitivity and therefore of his capacity to experience and worship God and serve his fellow men. Rollo May writes:

> It is a strange thing in our society that what goes into building a relationship—the sharing of tastes, fantasies, dreams, hopes for the future, and fears of the past—seems to make people more shy and vulnerable than going to bed with each other. They are more wary of the tenderness that goes with psychological and spiritual nakedness than they are of the physical nakedness in sexual intimacy.[2]

This tendency is immediately related to religious experience through a kind of new puritanism which has developed:

> I define this puritanism as consisting of three elements. First, a state of alienation from the body. Second, the separation of emotions from reason. And third, the use of the body as a machine. In our new puritansim, bad health is equated with sin. Sin used to mean giving in to one's sexual desires; now it means not having full sexual expression.[3]

And what, specifically, even from the purely natural viewpoint, is the main damage to the personality of this attitude? "This is the chief criticism of the new puritanism: it grossly limits feelings, it blocks the infinite variety and richness of the act, and it makes for emotional impoverishment."[4]

Facing this situation frankly will at least have the advantage of showing us the necessity of re-examining our relationships with our fellow men, of asking ourselves what we are doing to deepen our awareness of them as persons of mysterious depths, to be approached with reverence for their total being and total destiny; of asking ourselves what we are doing towards committing ourselves to others and to God. For we are not going to overcome the effects of our alienation and solitude or find our true identity and destiny by substituting part of the mystery of our being for the whole.

At this point it will be well to recall the other elements in our culture which make for affective starvation, things we talked about earlier in this book, and especially in Chapter 2: social mobility; the deadening effects of the machine; the depersonalization resulting from the immense growth of organizations—all having their effects in the breakdown of family life and of community. To all that we have said, two other matters of importance should be added here: conformism and the limitations of formalized worship when it is not supplemented by other forms of religious experience.

In the degree that people have lost a sense of their own self-identity and worth, they lean more heavily on the support of their environmental group, be it constituted by blood relationship, neighborhood, work, culture or whatever. And the more identity is found in the group, the greater is the pressure for conformity on the part of the members with regard to a way of thinking and talking—indeed with regard to a whole life style. The group cannot endure the upsetting effect of anyone who dares to be different. Needless to say, the effect of this pressure towards conformity is to repress the feelings of the individual, so that his self-expression is frustrated and inhibited. Happily, in our times there is more and more vocal protest against this unnatural tyranny.

In regard to formal worship, there will always be a place for the majesty and beauty of corporate adoration, reparation, thanksgiving, and petition both as a sign of our oneness in the one covenant Mediator, Christ our God, and as an informed and rightly intentioned help towards deepening that oneness. Besides, where there is a problem of serving large numbers with limited facilities and personnel, then large communities at worship, if they are already accustomed to feel themselves and to function as a natural community and a Christian fellowship, can profitably experience God, satisfy deep religous needs and, at the same time, accomplish the essential purpose of worship, which is to render homage to God.

But taking ourselves where we are and where we are likely to be in the immediate future, lacking the normal affective supports of a stable environment as well as many affective outlets and satisfactions, we are led to the need of supplementing formal worship with other kinds of informal worship in small groups, preferably in a homelike atmosphere. Bible-prayer groups are one way of providing such a supplement. Perhaps cultural changes will develop others equally effective.

In any case, several social currents are moving which make for the restoration of the affective to its proper balance in life and which therefore augment the fullness of man's experience of God as well as the possibility of more stability in religious experience. One thing is the movement towards the formation of communities. Even though, percentage-wise, the few thousand communes and colonies that already exist do not change the way of life for the vast majority, they are symbols that have meaning beyond their numbers. While some doubt their stability because they are contrary to contemporary culture, others say with just as much truth that precisely because they are a counter-culture and have rejected the values and ways of their surroundings, they are less likely to be affected by corrosive forces. What matters is their value in satisfying essential human needs, and their religious orientation. Generally speaking, communes with a religious leaven, now as in earlier times, are more stable.

To be of value, community has to have substance and depth. It has to begin with respect for the uniqueness of each person involved, respect for his rights, and the duty of respecting both the rights of the individual and the common rights of the group. It requires just the right balance between creative freedom in each member and a certain intensity of communal feeling that will keep searching for new ways both to express community and to increase it. The degree and kind of communication depends on the group and its members. It may depend as much upon nonverbal expression as upon words, for words at best are only another kind of symbol.

Words which are poetry have rich affective implications, and it is part of the whole movement towards the affective that poetry is again returning to its normal place in our culture. Nonverbal signs and experiences of unity such as are found in music and in the appreciation of beauty of every sort, whether in nature or in art, can also forge affective bonds. Man has an inescapable need for symbols and signs.

It is encouraging that in our time more and more people have the courage to write and to sing the songs that are real to them, songs which express an authentic human or religious experience. The power of such songs to evangelize in the best sense of the word—that is, to proclaim the good news that man has a Savior who has redeemed him—is very close to biblical prophecy, for they proclaim the message of the Lord to our times in a way that gets a hearing. The truth is one, but its many aspects are continually being discovered and given fresh expression out of the richness of the human heart. This is not to say, of course, that every writer of religious songs is anointed and commissioned by the Lord—far from it, given the mediocrity, or worse, which accumulates in songbooks. But there is deep truth in the observation of Andrew Fletcher, several centuries ago, that if a man were permitted to make all the ballads, he need not care who should make the laws of a nation. The songs of Israel, the Psalms, embodied divine teaching, sustained the faith of God's people under trial. They were in Our Lord's time the prayer of himself and his Mother, and in our own time they endure, to enlighten, inspire, and strengthen us.

Creative freedom grows through everything that is done to restore, protect, and promote man's awareness of himself, of other people, of nature, and of the rich possibilities of his own life. In religion today, fortunately, there is an increasing acceptance of the need and the rightness of experiencing God's concern with the total person he made us to be and whom he made to seek him with our total person—mind, will, emotions, and physical being. Our total worship and service must spring from, and ultimately embody, our whole self. To bring this total gift of self to God is the product of a lifetime of growth. Meanwhile what we need to develop, in creative freedom, is an increasingly sensitive response to the whole of experience, so that we shall be able to respond, from moment to moment, with originality and energy in service and love. Whatever awakens, expresses, or intensifies disciplined feelings makes a person more balanced, authentic, and productive.

A most felicitous expression of the truth for our time is the contemporary slang phrase "Jesus is in." He is in and with and among us with all his power and love, present and at home in this culture as in every other. His arm is not shortened. He has bound Satan, and all the resources of the modern world are at his command. He remains man's destiny, containing in his perfect manhood the perfection of all the natural tendencies of man. God is at work through the best in man, helping it to reach fulfillment despite everything in the world which would hinder the continuing process of redemption.

And the Holy Spirit, too, is "in," the Comforter, bringing his gifts of wisdom and knowledge and understanding; enabling man to rediscover the capacities of his own being; helping him to be open to the Spirit's transforming power; and, finally, bringing peace and joy. The Spirit-filled person is happy in all the fruits of "love, joy, peace, patient endurance, kindness, generosity, faith, mildness and chastity" (Gal 5:22). Towards this fullness of being the Holy Spirit is moving men by moving them away from excessive individualism towards community; from man-centeredness towards biblical commitment; from excessive activism towards prayer; from the cultivation of a self-image in "good works" to a service-orientated experience of Christ and other men; and from an arid intellectualism in religion towards a worship involving the donation of the whole person to God.

[1] *Love and Will* (New York: Norton, 1969), pp. 29, 31.
[2] Ibid., p. 45.
[3] Ibid.
[4] Ibid., p. 48.

CHAPTER 20

Personality Balance
and Self-Realization

Already in the Old Testament God revealed the wisdom of balance in our lives when he said in Prv 30:8-9: "Put falsehood and lying far from me, give me neither poverty nor riches; lest being full, I deny you, saying, 'Who is the Lord?' or being in want, I steal, and profane the name of my God." St. Paul knew the wisdom of keeping a balanced readiness for whatever may happen. "I am experienced in being brought low, yet I knew what it is to have an abundance. I have learned how to cope with every circumstance—how to eat well or go hungry, to be well provided for or do without. In him who is the source of my strength I have strength for everything" (Phil 4:12-13).

Practical experience indicates the need for humility and compassion in our understanding of ourselves and others. Nobody is perfectly balanced with regard to everything and everybody. And however well-balanced we are, we remain very vulnerable. A person who is normally poised and self-controlled may be dominated by emotion under severe strain, after prolonged frustration, or as the consequence of some accident which throws his whole life into disorder. Continuous association with disturbed people can erode the emotional health of the normal person—and there are other environmental factors of this kind. Above all, a person who is normally balanced and objective towards most people can be dominated by excessive feelings in his relationship with a particular individual.

It is very important for us to understand that the spiritual life is not meant to supersede the life of the natural man but to be built upon nature as a foundation. There are those who have come to the realization of this late in life. After twenty or even thirty years of trying to master themselves and be open, fully dedicated servants of God, they have very little to show for the struggle. Now they find that what they should have concerned themselves with in the first place was human growth—growth as human persons. Unaware of the extent to which emotional imbalance was thwarting them, they have been baffled all these years by the problems they were unable to resolve—personality conflicts, difficulty in concentrating during prayer, tensions which troubled them both in collaboration and in recreation with others. What was lacking was the natural basis of spiritual and apostolic growth.

This does not, of course, mean that prayer is not a mighty factor in our human growth. Keeping the thought of God at the center of life releases the energies of thought and will and clarifies the action whereby we move closer to him. The vital question here is the direction of our prayer: towards God and away from preoccupation with self. Such prayer begins with the acceptance of our human vulnerability and with the confidence that God is ready to help us in the right use of all our natural gifts.

It is sometimes said that women are more emotional than men. And it is usually a man who says it, intending it as a compliment to a supposed male superiority in this aspect of personality. But he deceives himself: the person who thinks of himself as unemotional is precisely the one most likely to become the victim of his own feelings. This explains a great deal of professional jealousy among men as well as women. Those who handed over Jesus for the death sentence "out of jealousy" (Mk 15:10) were men.

When we describe man as a rational animal, we are saying that he has the thoughts and will-acts of a spirit and the images and emotions of an animal. But he is neither angel nor animal.

In animals emotion is a concrete momentary response to a stimulus—food, danger. But man's every action is a human action: it is the response of his total personality—mind, will, and emotions, with the ability to remember the past, reason about the present, and foresee the future. To pretend that feelings are not an integral and important part of the human person is a disastrous error. We have already dealt with the social dimensions of this problem. Our concern here will be rather with the personal dimensions.

The people who come closest to living according to reason (granting that many of their objectives are above the reasoning of the natural man) are the saints—not that they are unemotional; on the contrary, they have gained the mastery of very strong emotions. The sense in which they live according to reason is that their lives are ordered by what they believe. But even while saints grow towards greater perfection and fullness of Christian personality, they must still wrestle with their own limitations and inner contradictions, some of which they will bear to the end of their lives.

The average person is more influenced by feelings than by reason. There are individual differences in the quickness of emotional response, the depth of feeling, and how long feelings last. Feelings are the spur to action—a person quite without emotions would lie in bed like a sack of potatoes. Feelings are involved in everything we do. The let-down, empty feeling we have after a celebration that has involved days of preparation and considerable activity is more than muscular tiredness; it is also a kind of psychic exhaustion.

To return to the question of whether women are more emotional than men: they do differ somewhat in the way they react emotionally because of the delicate, intimate, and in many ways mysterious union of mind, will, and body in the human person. It is possible to say this even though there are great differences between one man and another and one woman and another: this is called temperament.

Taken by and large, this seems to be true of feminine emotions. In women, the response is usually quick, but it is often brief. They are adaptable and tend to adjust quickly (and hence are less inclined to ulcers). God made women that way because a mother needs a quick and instinctive response to the multitudinous demands of family life, for the care of children who differ in age, temperament, intelligence, tastes, and so on. Women are emotionally equipped for teaching, nursing, social work. They are the apostles of the immediate. And since emotions fix on particulars, women have a great capacity for details and detailed work.

In men—taken, again, by and large—the response of feeling is usually slower, but once aroused it goes deeper and lasts longer. (In the days of dueling it was said that women could start men fighting but could not stop them—and the result was one less man in circulation.) Instead of adjusting quickly, men tend to fight opposition, resent it, and worry until something gives. Often what gives is part of their physical estate: they get ulcers or have a heart attack. God made men slower in their responses so that they could stand the rigors of fierce competition in life without wasting energy on little frictions, disappointments, and incidental preferences. Men have those deep and lasting emotions to sustain them in the economic arena and in the fight to bring large issues to victory. (In their personal lives, of course, men have their share of deep attachments to little things connected with food, personal comfort, hobbies and the like.)

What matters in both men and women is, of course, a healthy balance which makes for a fundamental peace and is the natural root of Christian growth. Without this balance, the very intensity of effort to achieve growth may take all sorts of odd and ridiculous forms and produce attitudes which amount to obsessive compulsions. This is because emotions fix on particulars and blow them up out of all proportion.

In men and women alike, maturity and balance mean largely emotional maturity. A child can be very intelligent, but accurate judgments in certain directions depend on experience and the increase of information. An adult who does not have emotional balance is simply an intelligent child (or an unintelligent child) who never matured. What degree of emotional control is necessary for personality balance? The answers are as different as are personalities. But there are guidelines that can at least help self-understanding and self-realization.

Emotional control means such a moderation of feelings that they will be neither less nor greater nor more enduring than the situation calls for. Its purpose is to make emotions our servants. Emotions are good servants, but they are very bad masters because they are blind and hence capable of wreaking havoc with our lives. Emotional maturity is essentially habitual emotional control.

It is immediately evident that emotional control is easier to define than to practice, and the difficulties are increased by the new permissiveness of our culture. For what formerly was decided by stable social values and manners must now be a matter of personal decision in many areas, with the inevitable result that a great and inescapable responsibility of self-restraint is placed on the individual. This demands habitual mastery of the inner dynamics of personality as he responds to stimulation from many directions.

Since we are dealing with forces which are basically orientated to serve the good of the whole person, it is well to start with what is right about them. First, emotion releases the energies we give to prayer, and the joy we experience in harmonizing our being and living with God's will adds impetus to our spiritual progress. Even at the natural level, people of great achievement are those who have learned to concentrate their emotional energies into driving power towards the goal they long for.

We have already said that our feelings enter into everything we do, and this is especially true of our relations with others. Emotion adds warmth and power to all our communication with others, facilitates the passage of our thought from the inward sphere of ourselves to the inward sphere of the other. It gives sympathetic understanding and gentleness, combined with a sometimes necessary forcefulness, in any exercise of authority. And everyone does have an authority of one kind or another, whether over one person or a thousand. So everyone needs to be sensitive, and sometimes strong, in reacting against what is wrong and correcting what should be corrected. At the same time, sensitive feelings make a person quick to respond to suffering in another, whether physical or spiritual, and prompt in action to relieve distress.

While no part of life can be lived in a continuous glow of emotion and friendship cannot depend on such a state, emotional response is an important part of friendship and of living up to the responsibilities of friendship. Every bond of shared idea, taste, or experience, every revulsion or attraction shared, is deepened and strengthened by the emotional resonance one friend discovers in the other.

Well-ordered emotions bring peace within which it is possible to keep alive that precious sense of wonder that God gives us as our natural heritage, to be discovered during childhood and brought to perfection in our adult years. The brutal overstimulation to which we are exposed in our present culture makes it all the more urgent that we should protect and rightly channel this precious part of our personality. God put great depth, richness, and goodness in persons and things, even in the simplest things. Much of our happiness in life depends on our ability to appreciate little things. It would be comic, if it were not tragic, to see the people knocking themselves out in the pursuit of uncontrolled desires for what the world thinks of as the good things of life, and all the while overlooking the simple but deep satisfactions that are always at hand.

To the saints and to the great, nothing is little because they are big enough to discover meaning and depth in the least of things. Jesus himself showed his sense of wonder at the innocence of children, the beauty of the lilies of the field. Saints like John of the Cross and Teresa of Avila, Francis of Assisi and Thérèse of Lisieux, all were remarkable for this affective sensitivity to everything about them.

God speaks in everything, and this sense of wonder is essentially an acceptance of the whole reality about us. Feeling helps to sustain and prolong our experience of its variety, beauty, and richness. There is no love between persons—husband and wife, parent and child, friend for friend—which is not deepened and stabilized by this response of our whole being to the real.

Emotion out of control, on the contrary, is in conflict with reality, and out of the inner disorder come anxieties and tensions and the whole toll of physical and mental disabilities which characterize the alienated person. Forty percent of the people who go to doctors have nothing organically wrong with them, and another twenty percent have troubles that are partly functional and only partly organic. Nevertheless it is true that the symptoms—pain, nausea, dizziness and the like—are all too real.

Achieving emotional balance in adult life, or regaining it if it has been lost, can be a crucifixion, but it is worth the pain. If one must suffer, let it at least be a suffering incidental to progress towards balance, freedom, and happiness. If our malaise is sufficiently grave, a great part of the pain—and the healing—must come from bringing into consciousness what has been hidden in the unconscious from our earliest years. For this we shall need skilled assistance. But there are many ways in which most of us can help ourselves.

It should be noted at once that pure repression is false spirituality because it is based on false information. Feelings out of control that are merely repressed do not disappear but rather gain strength: they cannot be turned off like a faucet or a light. If only repressed, they break loose from, or extend beyond, the original cause or occasion and pervade the whole personality, showing up in all sorts of aggressive or withdrawal symptoms and/or psychosomatic disturbances.

Repressed anger is an example. Suppose you have clashed with someone, and the encounter has left you burning with resentment, and with a sense of being grievously misunderstood. If possible, the misunderstanding should be cleared up at once; for the longer the situation continues, the more emotion will add fuel to your thoughts. But it is not always possible to "have it out" with the person in question. Nevertheless the energy released by your negative feelings has to be rechanneled in positive directions. This can be done in several ways: by concentrating on thinking understandingly and compassionately about the person who has offended you; by reasoning about the relative unimportance of the affair and, having put it in perspective, laughing at yourself a little for taking it so seriously; by doing something to show your good will towards the person; by considering both the other person and the situation as belonging to God's will for you at the present time and seeing God's love in them.

As in the case of anger, so with our other emotions. Everything that can be done to give feelings their normal, healthy, God-intended outlets will make it less likely that they will get out of control at unexpected moments. To dry up normal affections, either by a false asceticism or by the kind of total preoccupation with work which leaves normal sociability out of account, hinders our capacity to serve God and our fellow men with affection. Our affectionate relations with family and friends, our warm concern for the needs of others, our relaxed participation in various forms of recreation—all these things help to keep personality in balance.

Wherever there is a reasonable openness and freedom of discussion, it serves a most beneficial purpose of healing; it is really group therapy. Then there is the help one person can give another: when we are able to talk something over with a prudent person who is not emotionally involved and can reflect back the objective truth.

Of course, it is important that we should have deep convictions with regard to the value of restraint, when we are trying to keep ourselves on an even keel, avoiding depression or unfounded elation. Here, reading will help, from Scripture or some other inspirational source.

Finally, above all, prayer—whether formal or informal, in a church building or at home, liturgical or private—will help us to relate our total person to God. Prayer is often accompanied by a healthy emotional resonance. This is not to say that worship is to be used for an emotional binge, it is only to state the God-given harmony between the spirit and the body.

Needless to say, there can be no place for self-pity in a balanced personality, and we should avoid making too much of our difficulties. Living calmly in the real world, one day at a time, accepting the things that cannot for the moment be changed and wholeheartedly giving oneself to the work or enjoyment at hand, keeps affective energies moving within right channels. We shall not be able to dispel anxieties completely, and anyone who is trying to gain, or regain, control over fears must eventually face the painful duty of doing some of the things he is afraid to do.

Whatever we may do to achieve personality balance and self-realization at the natural level, we still take these terms within their limits and know that they can be interpreted in many different ways. Full self-realization can only be at a higher level; but, as we have said, a right balance at the natural level is normally essential to further growth. What can never be left out of account is the possibility of divine intervention to heal a person of emotional imbalance.

At any rate, words are sometimes used so loosely that they flap. "Maturity" is a case in point. Actually, maturity is a continuous development: it is not something we come to at some magical moment and stay in for the rest of our lives. There is a maturity proper and possible to every stage of life. And it can be lost. We are mature and realistic when we are very much aware of other people, of our surroundings, of moods and undercurrents; when we have humor, taste, appreciation, and humility —qualities which make other people feel important and bring out the best in them. We are mature when we are still teachable, quick to learn, flexible, ready to try a new thing, open to experience, willing to become involved in a good cause.

So it is not age but insight and adaptability that make for maturity. Maturity means having an inner sense of freedom that makes us independent of calendar years and of false perfectionism and lets things happen in God's own good order while we make the most of everything as a fresh experience to be assimilated and perhaps mastered. Maturity is a willingness to accept the fact that we are neither perfect nor hopelessly imperfect but always becoming. It is the awareness that we are neither quite so wonderful nor quite so hopeless as we once believed. It is making peace between what is and what might be.

So maturity is not so much a destination as a road. The rules and formulas help only a little. There are some signposts, such as we have indicated. Others might be added: Resilience, i.e., picking ourselves up after a setback and knowing that we have not disintegrated but are still quite intact. Discovering that someone else can do our job as well as we can, and going straight on doing it ourselves. Doing something we have always been afraid to do. Coming to realize that in our innermost being we are forever distinctively and uniquely ourselves, and therefore a bit lonely, sometimes quite a bit. So is everybody else. In this realization we are in some strange way more than ever together again with everybody.

One thing is certain: the emotionally balanced and mature person is not one who experiences no conflicts, tensions, or anxieties. The person who experiences no suffering, physical or mental, is a corpse. He should be buried. Real maturity is the ability to face the brutalities of life, to suffer a few battle wounds and live with a little scar tissue. And the higher a man's aspirations, the greater must be his capacity for pain.

CHAPTER 21

Friendship and Community

There is no one so much alone as the person alone in a crowd. This is the dilemma of urban man. He is crowded into trains, buses and subways, into offices, stores and factories, into neighborhoods, schools and apartment houses. Television and radio bring the restless life of mass civilization into his home. He feels the impact of this as a kind of pressure under which many of the humane pursuits of a fully civilized life are crowded out. Perhaps the aspect of life which suffers most is the affective communication which should exist between fellow human beings.

Not even the family can guarantee the intimacy of hearts which it should. Who does not know families in which parents and children are like islands, one isolated from another, each enclosed in himself and unhappy? It is not that there is nothing to talk about. Minds have been filled, and information can be exchanged off the top of the head. But the world seems to have crowded into all their lives, and personal openness is lacking in their relationships. Inevitably the conflict between the educated mind and the starved heart disturbs the personality and hinders the capacity to relate deeply with God or men.

Many families, of course, flee to the suburbs; but the chances are that they find there many of the features they have abhorred in city life—only more time must be spent in transportation.

Now, having stated this problem, we need not despair. We

have great resources at hand to solve it. What we must do is apply ourselves to studying the psychosocial conditions in modern life that cause disharmony between intellectual and affective development. Our thinking and planning must include both an understanding of the general problem of affective starvation and a practical program for forming children in families and in schools to seek and find affective satisfaction. Any real change is likely to come from a combination of our awareness of our deep human needs and an alertness which profits from both the stable and the changing currents of the environment.

Perhaps we should take as our starting point the human relationships which fall within our sphere as individuals. Thinking of our daily life, one thing that stands out is the extent to which apathy characterizes the crowds we see on urban streets, in offices, stores and so on. Could we not be, each of us, a beginning of change if we tried to bring to our personal encounters during the day a certain amount of warmth? Suppose we are asking for information: it is an error to suppose that such an interchange is exclusively intellectual. Even while head speaks to head, heart is also speaking to heart. Can we not communicate with this person by at least a friendly manner?

Sometimes the friendliness will seem to be all on our side. The affective capacity, the emotional depth and intensity, of persons differ. Unfortunately, in many people hidden emotional conflicts drain away affective energy, and their ability to come out of themselves and communicate with others is limited. But though they may seem wrapped up in themselves, we are not to infer that this is due to excessive self-love—indeed, the contrary is more likely the case. Well, we may feel that we have got no response; but it is impossible to tell, from so brief an encounter, the extent to which we have relieved that person's sense of isolation. And when, in some other, more fortunate individual, there is a response, this is the beginning of the kind of casual friendships which make a neighborhood into a community.

To move on now to the question of the necessity of love in human life: the saints have warned us that if we withhold our love from our fellow men we diminish our capacity for loving

God. And it is a fairly common experience that through a genuine love of friendship a person finds himself able both to experience the love of God more vividly and to respond to it more fully Ignace Lepp writes further:

> Frequently a man's passionate love for a woman increases his capacity to love God, his parents or friends—all renewing his creative élan. On the other hand, we have had occasion to note in a number of cases that when a man achieves an authentic love for God or mankind his capacity for erotic love increases proportionately. But an abuse of emotional energy in a given domain has harmful consequences for the totality of emotional life. Libertinism considerably inhibits creativity and relationships to the human community and to God.[1]

In the modern world all the affective relationships between persons have suffered from the attrition of a cultural decline, but perhaps the love of friendship has suffered most. To some extent, this is due to the pressures we have been discussing in this book: there is so little time, so little energy left over from the struggle for economic security and advancement —above all, so much moving from place to place. In part, the very nature of friendship makes it seem dispensable, for it is the least instinctive, organic, biological, or strictly necessary of the affective relationships. It is possible to beget and raise a family without friendship, and in our society it is sad to observe that this often happens.

The new morality, too, has had its role. Libertinism, as Ignace Lepp has noted above, inhibits creativity and relationships to the human community. Moreover, an ill-assimilated Freudianism has propagated the notion that all affection and tenderness is simply a disguise for frustrated sexuality, and the rise of open and explicit homosexuality has done much to render intimate friendship between members of the same sex suspect. The fact is that we live in a psychologically disturbed age in which the role of sex in human life has become distorted and the spiritual aspects of love too often lost sight of. We may safely say that too few people rightly value friendship because too few really experience it. This is a great misfortune for society, because far from being rooted in an unwholesome sexuality the love of friendship is the strongest spiritual bond of human fellowship. Without the love of friendship as a strong tide, neither the family nor the community can be secure or creative.

It cannot be overemphasized that Christianity is historically situated. Thus, while its central teaching contains the truth concerning the nature and destiny of man, this truth is only imperfectly reflected in a culture we call Christian. In every age, Christian spirituality experiences the impact of the forces in the culture which Christianity must leaven. So, during the first centuries, when the prevailing philosophy was Platonism, with its idealism and its view of the soul as the prisoner of the body—and inevitably as a reaction against the sensual excesses of paganism— Christian writers exalted the spirit over the body. While St. Thomas' synthesis of Plato and Aristotle issued in Christian realism on the philosophical and theological level, there was not, historically speaking, a corresponding development of psychology and of the respective roles of body and spirit. As a consequence, the excessive esteem for the rational, intellectual, and spiritual involved a belittling of the roles of the emotions in Christian spirituality.

At the opposite extreme from the first centuries is the culture which environs the Christian community today, with its downgrading of the rational, intellectual, and spiritual and accentuation of the sexual considered at the level of animal instinct. The fact is that however the problem of the body-soul relation is resolved philosophically, the problem which faces man in every age is that of the deformation of his power to love: so in every age the Christian community must reestablish Christian norms by returning to its sources.

In this matter of friendship, there are other dangers in modern society. Friendship is undervalued by those who have greater regard for the group than for the individual. The extreme case, of course, is totalitarianism. Among the Marxists, the party and the common struggle must have first place; the dictates of the party must be obeyed even though it means the betrayal of friends. Marxism creates a closed community, and to break with the party is to lose all friends within the party. But there is even a sense in which the democratic society, in principle so

216 THE EXPERIENCE OF GOD

favorable to the growth of friendship, can be hostile to it—when the democratic sentiment is carried to such lengths that friendship with a select few is seen as exclusiveness. This is a misunderstanding, of course, for friends stand shoulder to shoulder and serve interests beyond themselves in collaboration with others.

To return to the connection of friendship with erotic love, on which we touched briefly above: it is, of course, possible to experience erotic love and friendship for the same person. But in a certain sense nothing is less like friendship than erotic love. Lovers talk a lot about their love for each other, whereas friends rarely speak of their friendship. Lovers normally think of themselves as being face to face, absorbed in one another. Friends are side by side, absorbed in some common interest that goes beyond themselves. Above all, erotic love, while it lasts, is generelly something between two people, since it is the mutual surrender of the total person. By contrast, two, far from being the number necessary for friendship, is not even the best. It is rather only the beginning, since all true friendship is love that awakens and expands the richness of personality and is always directed towards the community.

So at this point it is in place to ask, "What does friendship presuppose in the personality?" First, there are certain likenesses and communications of common interest. The degree of similarity will depend in part on the degree in which personality is developed: those who are limited in their intelligence, affectivity, education, and experience will require in others more likeness to themselves in personal qualities, interests, opinions, beliefs, and social background if they are to be at ease and to communicate with facility. (This is true at the natural level. In a genuine fellowship of the Holy Spirit centered in God's word and in response through prayer, natural qualifications matter little. The affective bond is strong and warm and there is communication in depth about essential things.)

Persons of superior intelligence, wide experience, and emotional balance and depth are capable of establishing affective relationships with others very different from themselves, communicating with them at a deep level through interests held in common. So there are friendships between believers and atheists, Catholics and Marxists, and between persons who differ widely with respect to age, profession, or social conditions. Each is aware, in such circumstances, of the differences in the other as well as of the qualities which attract him.

But the unconscious also has its part. Perhaps at once, perhaps after some time, people will glimpse similarities in each other and their hearts will feel attracted. And at times, each sees intuitively not only what the other is at the moment but also what he is capable of becoming, perhaps owing precisely to their friendship. If either or both are aware of profiting from the friendship, this does not mean that its motives are selfish. Naturally, each hopes to receive something from the other, but each also expects to give something. What matters is the companionship itself.

Friendship does not belong exclusively to any time of life: there can, and should, be friendships between children, adolescents, and adults; between marriage partners; between parents and children, children and teachers. Yet to some extent age affects one's availability for friendship and desire for it. Young adults naturally want to meet and dialogue with their own kind. But when they fall in love, even though they do not consciously despise friendship, the couple tend to become preoccupied with each other. Then a few years later, after marriage perhaps, they are seeking out their friends again. Adults, if they are wise, preserve their friendships as well as their marriage relationships, seeing both as indispensable to growth and happiness. How much time is given to one or the other will vary according to the personality of the individual and the changing circumstances of life. In any case, owing to their greater experience and development of personality, adults are more suited to friendship than adolescents: but they must keep themselves young in heart.

To be a friend one should desire not only the mutual support which friendship provides, but also common growth and development of personality and the outward-turning which embraces other members of the community. From this point of view, the differences between friends are worth as much as the likeness, the understanding of one being broadened by association with the other. But, as has been said, when there is an attraction towards a particular person, it is because one intuitively senses in him a certain likeness to oneself. Both sense a capacity to get along well with each other, feel that they might have much to say to each other. This intuition depends on our self-image—that is, on the self-ideal we would like to achieve—for this is the main influence directing our energies and our way of thinking and acting. (This is very different from the kind of moral egoism which seeks others as mirrors of itself and exploits them to reflect its own self-image. People like that are incapable of real friendhip.)

To put it more clearly: in making friends we intuitively look for someone who has in his personality at least some aspects of our own self-ideal; we are looking for the ideal of ourselves incarnated in our friend. Because of this, friends are people who are already alike and become more alike through the communication that goes on between them.

Sometimes friends discover each other through some purely accidental encounter, but generally friendship arises out of some sort of habitual association which permits the two to look below the surface to the essentials of personality. Among those with whom you are brought together through sharing the same religion, studies, occupation, or even recreation, you may suddenly discover another person who considers something important which has little importance for others—but you share his outlook on this matter. Thus a friendship is born.

More specifically, it might be said that friendship begins at the moment when someone makes a self-disclosure to us, and we sense that it is made at some cost and is in that sense an act of love. He shows that he cares enough to open himself to us even at the risk of rejection. And we reciprocate this act of love by risking the disclosure of our true self to him. Thus begins the interknowledge which deepens into that love of friendship which is based on sharing the same visions and goals, loving—and hating—the same things.

Since friendship begins with self-revelation there is no room in it for pretense, no need for the masks we wear for those lesser relationships with the variety of people with whom we are, perhaps, acquainted. Since it is founded in disinterested love, it is not possessive but wants the good of the friend. "A faithful friend is beyond price, no sum can balance his worth. A faithful friend is a life-saving remedy, such as he who fears God finds; for he who fears God behaves accordingly, and his friend will be like himself" (Sir 6:15-17). So it is that the marriage relationship is closer and stronger when these two people who love each other are also friends.

A true friend is a compassionate counselor to whom one can go with perfect confidence to seek advice and help in solving problems. A friend speaks with all frankness in correcting, encouraging, and advising. Everyone needs someone in whom he can confide. Sometimes a spiritual adviser or a professional will do, but not always, because the paternal relationship is not the same thing as the fraternal intimacy which belongs to friendship. What one needs at such times is an equal to whom one can talk with perfect liberty: but it must be a special person who will not betray one's confidence—in other words, a friend.

However, it must not be thought that friedship will consist of the incessant exchange of confidences. On the contrary, there is a sentimental kind of relationship which is to be avoided: the two are wrapped up in each other; they have been attracted to each other by superficial qualities, and the bond between them is the pursuit of pleasure. There is real danger here, because the search for selfish pleasure increases sensuality and what begins with the frivolous and sentimental easily becomes sensual. Friendships of this kind waste time and energy at best, and at worst end in tragedy. Not only do they hinder personal growth, but they also obstruct concern for others and fidelity to God. Nevertheless, if two persons have become involved in such a friendship, not all is lost. For although these relationships are largely instinctual and blind, they sometimes can, with good will and wise counseling, grow into something more beneficial for those concerned and for the community.

With regard to this matter of the exchange of confidence, mention should be made of a certain reserve which belongs to true friendship: friends do not seek knowledge of personal matters merely out of curiosity. This is the dignity of true friendship: each is left free to divulge what he will, when he will.

The bond which unites them essentially is a common love of something beyond themselves from which they gain strength. It is not that this common interest absorbs the friends so wholly that they forget each other; on the contrary, it is the means by which the friendship exists and functions; understanding and love are mutual. With each step towards the common goal the friend proves himself, and there is a growth on each side of respect, admiration, and love. Friends fight side by side, argue with each other if need be, work, read, pray, and live side by side.

True friendship is the least jealous of all loves. Indeed it is a mark of true friendship that it welcomes others who are like-minded into a widening circle of friends. In each of the friend-ships there is something that only the other friend can discover. No one person, by himself, has such depth of being that he can discover all the richness of another human person. And so the coming of others into the friendship makes other facets of one's friend shine brightly. In this sense we know that we possess our friend not less but more, in the measure that the number sharing the friendship increases. As Dante said, "Here comes one who is going to augment our love." It is because it is not carnal but a thing of the spirit that friendship can be shared with many without the part belonging to each one's being diminished.

Because it is of the spirit—that is, the stable element in the human person—friendship can withstand the tests of separation, aging, physical and intellectual change. For through all changes, accidental but nevertheless real, our most profound self remains identical. But it is a dynamic identity: we shall all keep changing until our death. So it is that friends meeting after a long separa-tion must reassess each other, and if it is a good friendship each brings the other something new, something developed in himself. Of course, if the friendship is to remain active, there must be contacts from time to time; otherwise it would become only a tender memory.

As friend is linked with friend and each friend has other links with other friends, so through all the friendships in a whole group the community is more extensively and intensively united within itself. So, as we have already pointed out in an earlier chapter, Christ worked with nature and not against it when he chose his first twelve from those who already had natural ties of kinship or friendship and the experience of working together. Yet there was failure among the twelve; there was one who betrayed him. So friendships within a group are always in danger of failure through jealousy, exclusiveness, or sensuality. This is one of the reasonable risks of life that must be realistically faced and accepted.

We spoke earlier of the necessity the Christian community has of constantly returning to the Christian norm of friendship. It is found in the most sublime words ever spoken about friendship, the words of Jesus, the perfect friend:

> This is my commandment: love one another as I have loved you. There is no greater love than this: to lay down one's life for one's friends. You are my friends if you do what I command you. I no longer speak of you as slaves, for a slave does not know what his master is about. Instead, I call you friends, since I have made known to you all that I heard from my Father. It was not you who chose me, it was I who chose you to go forth and bear fruit. Your fruit must endure, so that all you ask the Father in my name he will give you. The command I give you is this, that you love one another. (Jn 15:12-17)

[1] *Psychoanalysis of Love* (New York: Macmillan, 1966), p. 20.

CHAPTER 22

Committed Celibacy
in Spiritual Leaders

The heart of the affective life of man and woman is the sacred mating instinct of procreation. But there are those in the Christian community who, in response to a vocation from God, sacrifice the fulfillment of this instinct through a commitment to a celibate life. All that has been said of human affective needs and outlets, their influence on thinking and willing, their driving force and influence on personality, and the necessity of balance must be related to the understanding, the making, and the maintenance of a commitment to celibacy. Like married life, the life of celibacy calls for emotional maturity; but like marriage, the celibate life is usually entered by persons in whom maturity is not yet achieved: some imbalance exists in everyone in one degree or another. So the acceptance of dedication to an ideal must always be made by a person who falls short of the ideal.

This realistic human appraisal must also be put in the historical and social context which affects our thinking and our capacity to will the ideal. The depersonalization of modern technological civilization which produces affective starvation and creates a hunger for compensation; the abnormal preoccupation with physical comfort and pleasure in general; the overemphasis on sex and the tendency to identify all love with physical love—all these factors have been explored in earlier chapters. Only with regard to the last factor is further comment relevant here.

The whole thrust of advertising in our affluent society is to create needs in the consumer for the products. So with sex: in contemporary society the capacity has been lost to distinguish between sexual desires and sexual needs. People differ from one another in this respect, of course, but there is a great deal of evidence to indicate that although sexual desires are many, sexual needs are few. After three years of study at the Kinsey Institute, two psychologists published their conclusion that in itself the sex instinct is not strong but weak. The problem, they said, is created by the obsession with sex in the environment. Modern science thus corroborates a conclusion of long standing. "There is not much sinning because of natural desires," writes St. Thomas. "But the stimulations of desire which man's cunning has devised are something else, and because of these there is much sinning."[1]

This social climate that overstimulates an instinct which would otherwise be easier to regulate belongs to a historical development going back five centuries. It is not to extol the superior merits of a social order still barbaric in many ways to say that the life of the high Middle Ages was God-centered and that with the excesses which accompanied the naturalistic interest in the human body of the Renaissance began the development which would culminate in the total secularization of modern Western culture.

When the religious reformers of the sixteenth century insisted that priests and religious must marry, they were not so much concerned with the biological and psychological needs of the clergy as with protesting against the authority of the Church. Nevertheless it had the effect, in the turmoil of those times, of implying that celibacy was impossible and virginity without value. Thus, while the ideal and practice of celibacy was preserved in the Catholic Church, it was devalued in the environing culture of the Western world. At the same time, in the spiritual sphere, the following centuries witnessed the passing of men from the authority of God to the authority of self-sufficient human reason.

It is not to oversimplify the complex interaction of historical and economic forces to observe that following the industrial revolution there was a gradual descent from the man of reason to the physical man and to the machine. Is there not a real question today of the extent to which the authority of man is submitted to the authority of the computer? The present protest against a technology out of control was anticipated by Pius XII when he said, in a Discourse of October 21, 1947: "There must be some limit set to the dwarfing of man himself in these days through the emergence and dominance of the machine and the continued expansion of large-scale industry . . . . Therefore craftsmen as a class are, one may say, a picked militia defending the dignity and personality of the workman." As the Christian community endeavors to leaven contemporary post-Christian society, is there not an analogy, in the dedicated virginity which survives from the ancient world, of a picked militia defending the dignity and personality of the human being?

At the turn of the century, the German Protestant theologian Adolf von Harnack wrote:

> Any kind of community calls for some persons who devote them-
> selves exclusively to it. Thus the Church calls for volunteers who
> abandon every other calling and devote themselves wholly to the
> service of their neighbor, not because such a vocation is higher,
> but simply because it is necessary, and because such an impetus
> will necessarily come from a Church that is truly alive.[2]

So the Protestant community of Taizé, when after much deliberation they came to see that celibacy was necessary to their apostolate, found valid all the reasons given by St. Paul in 1 Corinthians 7:32-35—that is, greater availability to serve God and man and to be intent upon spiritual things. But they did not claim that celibacy puts anyone in a superior position in the eyes of God or with regard to salvation; for as Jesus himself said: "None of those who cry out, 'Lord, Lord' will enter the kingdom of heaven but only the one who does the will of my Father in heaven" (Mt 7:21).

To turn from the Christian West to the East: Mahatma Gandhi, after several years of married life, decided in his thirties to renounce the use of marriage and live as a celibate. It was an extremely difficult decision to reach, and only after returning to his wife several times did he succeed in making the break final. But he made his choice with his wife's consent in order to dedicate his total energies to his social apostolate of liberating the oppressed. It is hard to question the added effect that committed celibacy had on his apostolate.

Today young Christian laymen and laywomen, as in former times, are making the decision to commit themselves to celibacy for the sake of serving God and man with greater availability and undivided concern. The value they place on this life, however, in no way reflects on the sacredness or the necessity of marriage for the majority of men and women. It is only to recognize what most married people would surely admit very readily, i.e., that the greater part of their time and energy is taken up with the care of their families. This is not meant to disparage the excellent work done by the married clergy of various denominations. Obviously God chooses them to do great good among untold numbers of people. The question is one of a different vocation.

It is a time for great tolerance and mutual understanding with regard to differences in vocation. It should be recognized that there is an extraordinary need in the world today for the undivided life of the celibate. Even with no responsibilities apart from his apostolate, he finds himself with far more work immediately at hand than he can possibly accomplish within his human limits. If it is suggested that his celibate way of life might impede his understanding of human needs, it should be noted that the very breadth and depth of his apostolate keeps him so constantly among people and so constantly at their immediate service that there is no sense of separation from them as human beings but only the detachment which permits the total dedication of his energies to a spiritual ministry to many. It is no barrier to service, or to respect and love, that he should remain somewhat apart in his relation to God; quite the contrary: "Every high priest taken from among men is appointed for men in things pertaining to God, that he may offer gifts and sacrifices for sins. He is able to have compassion on the ignorant and erring, because he himself also is beset with weakness, and by reason thereof is obliged to offer for sins, as on behalf of the people, so also for himself" (Heb 5:1-4). It belongs to his Christian vocation that he is at once, mysteriously, detached from and very close to people.

We live in a world in which human suffering has reached massive proportions, and concern for liberation of the poor and the oppressed must be a vital part of the apostolate. Yet if the special calling of the picked milita of committed celibates and virgins is to defend the dignity and personality of men and women, the service of their spiritual needs must be primary; now as in every age and circumstance this is a mission which is irreplaceable.

Essential to an understanding of committed celibacy is the conscious dedication to this ideal, with or without a public, official ritual. That dedication is made in the heart of man, after preparation and deliberation. It is worship of a high order, for the commitment is made to God, normally in collaboration with fellow men, to serve divine purposes and to share with Christ his mission to redeem man. Through his dedication, the celibate enters into the divine order of action that through Christ reaches back to the beginning of sacred history and forward into eternity. He is not alone, nor does he act merely at the human level nor with merely human consequences and results. Jesus is at work through him, and vital contact with Jesus through prayer keeps him very much aware of this. "Your life is hidden now with Christ in God" (Col 3:3). "Christ will be exalted through me, whether I live or die" (Phil 1:20). "The life I live now is not my own; Christ is living in me. I still live my human life, but it is a life of faith in the Son of God, who loved me and gave himself for me" (Gal 2:20).

Since his dedication is worship, every restraint of chastity in living his commitment is worship offered in union with all the worshipping members of Christ. He is not standing alone with a personal problem but is with all his being joined to the worshipping Christian community where Jesus himself is the life and heart of all worship. We adore, thank, and plead in the name and by the blood of Jesus. Everything is through him. In every worshipper it is always Christ worshipping the Father through his brothers and sisters.

Moreover, through our oneness with Christ and through our being alive with the one Christ-life, we have implanted in us the power to join with Christ in putting his power into action, releasing his Holy Spirit into men's hearts, bringing men the friendship and joy of Christ and doing all the things that he promised believers would do. We are the sign of Christ's presence and saving power among men. Living his love and uniting with one another in our life and ministry, we become visible signs that the Father has truly sent Jesus to be our Savior, and that the Father loves us as he loves his Son.

More specifically, the commitment of the dedicated celibate is a sign of how completely his life has to be lived for God if he is to be the presence, power, love, and unity of God made visible among men. It is his personal commitment to God, to be lived directly for love of God so as to bear fruit that will endure. It is not to be lived for mere convenience nor to go through with a difficult bargain. It is a commitment that stands for his person, his deepest self. True to himself, he wants to honor his commitment. In fulfilling himself, he fulfills·also the needs of his fellow men and gives adoration to God.

The dedication of the celibate is also a sign of the transcendence and holiness of God, for it is a human way of saying that from him we receive all that we have and are. Before the infinite, unsearchable depths and might of God, we are nothing; everything comes to us as his gratuitous gift. We could never deserve the Christ-life which is ours; we could easily misuse it; and we can lose it if we do not fulfill the conditions of its possession. God is all, and before him we are only what he chooses us to be. Unless an awareness of this, and the dread of emptiness which it engenders, is a real experience in the depths of our being, we can never understand the human heart of Jesus when he said, "The Father is greater than I. I love the Father and do as the Father has commanded me. Come, then! Let us be on our way!" (Jn 14:28, 31). These were Jesus' words when he felt the dread of being man's Savior with the sins of the world upon him, saw before him the imminent necessity of suffering the holocaust of himself.

Since the transcendence and holiness of God merits our total giving, the commitment of the celibate, if he is a priest, must be stable and permanent. The unlimited duration of his giving is a sign of its completeness. Realistically made by an adult who has seen many changes go on around him and experienced many changes within himself, a commitment to celibacy takes for granted the continuance of change both within and without. However intense those changes, they remain accidental: they do not belong to the essence of himself. This is true even if, with the full awakening of manhood, they involve falling in love. The emotional impact of any experience can never be fully anticipated, and a problem becomes a problem at the moment mainly because emotion puts the mind in turmoil. But the essential person who existed before the impact of the experience will exist after it has ceased to disturb him. To be rational, a person committing himself to celibacy, as in committing himself to anything else, must accept the reasonable risks of life, with all its unpredictable changes, without excessive fear, without self-pity, and without hedging or reservations. He knows that God remains in control of his world, giving stability when men might waver or be tempted to desert. The important thing is to remain firmly united with the unchanging and unchangeable God by meditation on his living word and by prayer. Such a reinforcing of basic motives is necessary to perseverance in any commitment.

The stability of the committed celibate helps to stabilize all other Christian commitments, and especially the commitments of husband and wife to one another and to their children. This has added weight because, even if not priests, normally spiritual leaders are the ones who make the commitment. Their stability is at once the sign of their sincerity and a sign that the power of God which attends them can also come to the aid of anyone in the Christian community who feeds spiritually at the sources of the Mass, the sacraments, God's word, and prayer. Correspondingly, the instability of spiritual leaders has a notably unsettling effect on the Christian community, partly because it gives rise to disillusionment and despair and partly because it provides an excuse for infidelity among persons who are looking for one anyhow.

The stabilizing action of Christ is always through his priesthood functioning in and through his Christian community. The committed celibate participates with the Christian community in the purifying, strengthening, and spiritual rebirth of human love. He helps to stem the destructive abuse of the sacred mating instinct and thus to increase the fruitfulness of married love itself. He does this by his covenant-centered prayer, by the merits of his worship, works, and sufferings and his fidelity to his commitment. Moreover, those who live the celibate life are a source of strength to married people, as the latter are the first to acknowledge; for the completeness of the celibate's sacrifice inspires sacrifices. The example and ideal of lived celibacy thus becomes a moral cause of the chastity of the married; a moral cause, too, in the strengthening, stabilizing, and fructifying of the family community and the Christian community.

When the true meaning of the life of dedicated celibacy is seen, it becomes evident that it in no sense involves an impairment of manly or womanly personality. The Christian, living with the life of Christ, is called to manifest the human heart of Christ, the unique quality of his human love. Celibate and virginal chastity have a special power to symbolize the undivided heart of Christ in his disinterested love of men and his fidelity to the Father. The woman whose virginity is consecrated to God images the chastity, integrity, and fruitfulness of Mary. It may be, as we have said, that some people will bring immaturity to the commitment to celibacy. If so, it will present a problem; but the problem will not be greater than it would be in marriage, nor will the celibate life aggravate this difficulty more than would married life.

We have here no lasting city, and dedicated celibacy is above all a sign that there is a kingdom to come, that it is on the way, and that it is a break with the world as we know it. This life consecrated to God in time is a sign of the primacy of the spirit and a foreshadowing of what we shall be in the world to come when our mortal bodies experience the glorification which is the fullness of the risen life. "What is sown is perishable, what is raised is imperishable. It is sown in dishonor, it is raised in glory. It is sown in weakness, it is raised in power. It is sown a physical body, it is raised a spiritual body" (1 Cor 15:42-44, *RSV*).

The spiritual paternity of the celibate priest is a mirroring on earth of the divine paternity after which all paternity on earth is named. And so, far from being a devaluation of marriage, it is a guarantee of the sacred value of marriage and procreation as a way of life not imposed on the majority of men and women by a necessity of nature but willed by God for the service of Christ and his community.

VI

Conclusion

CHAPTER 23

The Prophetic Role
of the Redeemed Christian
in a Secular World

Modern man is caught in the tension between a God-given impulse towards progress and perfection, on the one hand, and on the other, a sense of guilt at some of the inhuman qualities and consequences of his forward movement. Does he take himself so seriously that he cannot stand the thought that there might be imperfection in himself or his works? In any case the present crisis has been long in coming. In earlier chapters of this book we have traced the long process of secularization which began with the Renaissance. The dynamism of modern technology is the culmination of the assertion by the secular of its own identity and meaning.

Secularity may be defined as "the march of mankind, in the autonomous light of its own resources, toward the mastery and humanization of the world."[1] But modern man is unhappy in what he has achieved and restless in his abundance. He is torn with inner conflicts, and searches, sometimes wildly, for innocence. Ironically, the very technological marvels he has achieved have given him the leisure and freedom to look critically at his accomplishments, and he has found problems that cry out for solution. Hence the protests of our day against "the establishment" which so often issue in violence, or in withdrawal from society. In either case, what is involved is a search for innocence.

Protest has a role, of course, in alerting men to the evils in society. But whether from the left or from the right, it contains the risk of becoming an end in itself. The confrontation of evil is only delayed by the primitive projection of unbearable guilt onto systems, classes, governments, universities. The bombshell technique, whether literal or psychological, is not constructive. We reform nothing by destruction or by abdication: purification and renewal must be organic and from within.

In this troubled secularized world in which the Christian inescapably lives, his role is the re-establishment of Christian norms. He is commissioned to live with great compassion for the wounds of his fellow men, collaborating with them freely and hopefully for the purification of man's magnificent achievement. And he is able to proceed patiently and optimistically because he has learned from the living word of God and from living experience both of the goodness of men and of the redeeming presence of God among them. He knows and respects the goodness and autonomy of nature, being aware that God has placed the goodness and autonomy in things and rarely intervenes in the operation of natural laws—indeed his miraculous intervention for the salvation of men only serves to emphasize the autonomy of the laws' normal operation and to hint that there are potentialities in nature which man does not yet know.

Playing his part in the scheme of redemption, the Christian is wrestling realistically with the age-old tensions between the city of God and the city of man, Christianity and civilization, Christ and culture, grace and nature. In resolving these tensions he lives creatively, rightly seeing his work in the world as a collaboration with the redemptive process and seeing the tremendous creativity of secular technology as a prolongation of, and a participation in, the creativity of God. And so the Christian comes as a prophet to reveal who God is, what nature is, and how man's destiny is to be worked out within the structures of the creation.

There is a sense in which our epoch of radical change has a great resemblance to the age of the Reformers. For whatever may have been the accidental historical occasions of dissent, the Reformation was largely a radical reaction to the new leap forward represented by the culture of the Renaissance. Let not the present-day Christian community repeat the mistakes of that time. The generation of Luther felt guilty because it was not caught up with the new emergence of the secular, because it happened without religious influence when they felt that religion should have shaped it. Unable to integrate the new scientific learning into religious culture, they felt that they must resist it as antagonistic to religion. The result was a cleavage between the sacred and the secular which ensuing centuries rendered more acute and which persists in Western civilization today.

The authentic Christian must confront the turmoil of the technological world that surrounds him with a patient understanding that all the fuss about structures is only a mask for the secular world's discontent with itself, not with respect to its achievement but with respect to its failure to attain its identity in relation to man, to the sacred, to the universe, and to God. The solution is not to confront enormous energies with enormous contempt but to bear patiently the attrition of modern life, identifying with our fellow men and helping them to recognize and accept both the truth of the secular and the truth of the sacred. For the secular is not something outside man; it is something which takes its origin from the depths of his being, and it is there that the reconciliation must be made; there that man must learn so to use the secular that it may, through him, come to its highest realization.

Old habits of thought will get in the Christian's way. Too often, until now, the religious man has held the secular suspect as secular. The secular has resisted criticism of its defects and reasserted its autonomy by attempting to demythologize the sacred, and theology has counterattacked by attempting to demythologize the secular and strip it of its self-divinization. While the Christian preserves the distinction between the sacred and secular and rejects the absolutes by which the secular world would divinize itself, he must be careful not to derogate its magnificence by treating it as a machine.

Since the undertaking whereby man strives to master the

world is a participation in God's continuing act of creation, it must be seen as spiritual. So the Christian is committed to the achievement of excellence in the secular sphere; and so likewise is he committed to furthering the emergence of the spiritual throughout the secular sphere by leaving the secular free to do its own work of exploring the human. Secularity must be allowed its autonomy and unconditionality so that everything in nature can emerge in its inner purpose, meaning, and identity in the total scheme of redemption. To reduce the secular to the sacred is as much a betrayal as to reduce the sacred to the secular. The growth of each and the harmony between them can be accomplished only by a great openness in each, for our understanding of God, of man, and of the world continues to grow. New insights are gained, new depths of truth revealed, as the secular strives to humanize itself and the sacred strives to bring itself into relation with the vast new secular world. Man lives in an open-ended world of many contingencies and possibilities, in an unexpected universe, and we should beware of premature conclusions.

Nevertheless the Christian must never become unaware of the possibilities for terror in our technological civilization; he must never relax his vigilance with regard to the threat to human values. Happily there is today a wholesome moral earnestness in the vision of many people, not only among leaders in science, education, business, and government but also in society at large. There is, as we noted earlier in this book, a thrust towards the rejection and correction of the defects and abuses in the treatment of human persons and of our natural environment. The Christian should take advantage of every natural community which offers hope of solid growth towards an authentic Christian community. He should employ to the full every medium—the press, radio and TV, forums, conferences and the like—for the presentation of Christian solutions to concrete social problems.

But the Christian still lives and works in a divided world at war with itself, and the Beatitudes summarize his condition. He is a prophet of the goodness of this world; he works with the best of men and with the best in every man as he tries both to accept the truth to which men are attaining by merely natural means and to lead them to a personal experience of God who is also a Savior present among them. The Christian can proceed with confidence, cultivating openness in himself and others, for he knows that the truth of the secular, if it is really true, will not contradict the truth of the sacred, since God is the author of both. In this he will be giving his fellow men an example of obedience to reality, a reality in which suffering has a place because there is no growth without suffering. And so the Christian will share with his fellow men that larger vision in which the goodness of everything in the created universe is seen, and man's capacity for redeeming the things he touches with his intelligence and good will; in which suffering is bearable because it carries forward the work of redemption wherein man has a destiny beyond himself.

The Christian is also the prophet of moderation among men. "Rejoice in the Lord always," writes St. Paul; "again I say, rejoice. Let your moderation be known to all men. The Lord is near" (Phil 4:4-6). The Greek word for "moderation" here means "forbearance," a willingness to give up one's rights. Christians must be moderate especially in their relations with their fellow men. This moderation is not instinctive, as in animals, but must be freely chosen. Free men must deliberately choose to be moderate in their love out of reverence for each unique person: they must never impose themselves either physically or emotionally. They must not make an idol of their own passions but transcend themselves in response to the call of a transcendent God to a destiny beyond themselves.

Men can violate things as well as persons through lack of moderation; they can plunder the resources of their environment, and in thus abusing things they do even greater violence to themselves. And so the Christian, by his moderation which in some will go to the length of voluntary poverty, will be in his way of life a prophet of moderation in the use of things. "Have no anxiety," St. Paul continues, "but in every prayer and supplication with thanksgiving let your petitions be made known to God. And may the peace of God which surpasses all understanding guard your hearts and your minds in Christ Jesus" (Phil 4:6–7). The peace and joy of the Christian (and

they are real even for those of us who are not saints) point
forward to the kingdom of God which is coming and is already on
the way; and so they are a sign to a world in which men have to a
great extent, perhaps, mastered the resources of nature but have
not sufficiently learned to revere and love them.

But the Christian cannot function or achieve his goals alone.
From the beginning God has addressed his saving message to
a community. In the depths of his being every Christian is related
and bound to every other in a community of love. And this
community, in turn, is committed to extend its gospel, its love,
and its saving power beyond itself to all men. It is, by commitment to the world's Savior, a prophetic community. Within it,
and never apart from it, the Christian carries out his prophetic
role in the secular world that is the culture of our time. In so
doing he will be running counter to many forces in the culture
of our time; it is so in every age.

Above all, the Christian will be a prophet in the secular world
with regard to the two missionary goals that Christ set before
his disciples so clearly: "This is how all will know you for my
disciples: your love for one another" (Jn 13:35). The world needs
to see a genuinely human community in which there is love.
"I have given them the glory you gave me that they may be
one, as we are one—I living in them, you living in me—that
their unity may be complete. So shall the world know that you
sent me, and that you loved them as you loved me" (Jn 17:22-23).
Whatever trials the age may bring to the faith of Christians,
the world needs to see the unity even in the face of diversity
of personalities and cultures, even in the midst of dissent and
debate, which is the mark of Christ's disciples. And as the community advances in the fulfillment of its saving history, it
advances also in the fulfillment of its humanity. Only a truly
human community can be also a Christian community. Only
a human and Christian community can be, in the liturgy of
the word and sacrifice, a Eucharistic community where Christ
is the living center, the Lord and Savior.

---

[1] William Lynch, *Christ and Prometheus* (Notre Dame, Indiana: University of Notre Dame
Press, 1970), p.7.